# Deep Roots

## Introduction

On the threshold of this poetic journey, where words are seeds and each verse a sprout, we delve into the garden of "Deep Roots". This book is a tribute to the earth, that generous mother who sustains and nourishes us, who teaches us the passion for life in each grain of her soil.

Here, among metaphors and Songs to the earth, we seek to unearth the very essence of our existence. Each poem is a song to life, an earthly embrace that connects us with the primordial force of our planet. With overflowing passion, we explore the invisible ties that bind us to the earth, those golden threads that weave our history and our future.

"Deep Roots" is more than a book; it is an experience, a feeling, a return home. Through its pages, I invite the reader to feel the pulse of the earth, to listen to its whispers and to celebrate the magnificence of life in its purest and truest form.

May this book be a refuge for the soul, a space where the passion for life blossoms in every word, and where, together, we can honor the eternal beauty of our common home: the Earth.


## Deep Roots


From the whisper of the leaves,
to the murmur of the rivers,
the earth sings in a thousand tongues,
its stories, its mysteries.
With roots that sink,
into the heart of time,
the earth stands firm,
source of life, temple.
Under the infinite sky,
the green mantle extends,
the earth is mother and home,
in her embrace, we shelter.
From the proud peaks,
to the serene valleys,
the earth is a living canvas,
of beauty, of dreams.
It is on the earth where we are born,
where we grow and learn,
with deep roots, we live,
and in the end, to her we return.

## A Song to the Earth

In the lap of the earth lies the sigh of time, where roots intertwine in an eternal embrace. It is here where the song is born, deep and sincere, a melody that rises, passionate and true.

The earth, with its emerald and ochre mantle, whispers stories of yore, of love and disdain. Each grain of its being, a testament to life, a legacy of nature, inviting us to understand.

Under the moon, silent witness to endless cycles, the earth sheds its veil, revealing its skin. With each twinkling star, a wish is sown, and in the darkness, hope blooms, faithful.

The sun, in its chariot of fire, brings the dawn of the day, bathing the world in light, in warmth, in energy. The earth awakens, stretches, expands, and in its awakening, life spreads, ignites.

The rivers, arteries of this planetary body, flow with the wisdom of the ages, a sanctuary. In their clear waters, the sky is reflected, and in their course, they carry promises to the sea, a longing.

The trees, sentinels of whispering leaves, stand proud, their branches dancing. Their roots, like veins, nourish from the earth, and in their embrace, remind us of our own era.

The mountain, majestic, defiant and serene, rises as an altar, where the earth commends itself. Its peak touches the sky, its base, anchored to the ground, and in its stillness, offers us a refuge, a comfort.

Thus, in each element, in each particle and in each being, the earth speaks to us, teaches us, asks us to believe. In its infinite goodness, in its strength, in its spirit, it shows us that life, in its complexity, is a rite.

May this book be a journey, a discovery, an exploration of the earth and its sacred breath. With "Deep Roots", I invite you to feel, to love, to live, and in the earth, to discover yourself.

And in the whisper of the breeze, the earth confides in us, its deepest secrets, its wisdom. It is a whisper that becomes a roar, a call to consciousness, a shared destiny.

The earth, with its scars and folds, tells us stories of resilience, of fires and snows.

It speaks to us of its pain, of its joy and its struggle, of how each being, in its bosom, finds its path.

In the heart of the jungle, where life intertwines, where the jaguar stalks and the orchid embraces, the passion of the earth manifests itself wild, in a perfect balance, an eternal journey.

The dunes of the desert, with their golden sand, invite us to reflect on life, on nothingness. It is a canvas of contrasts, of silence and calm, where the earth shows itself in its purest soul.

And so, in each grain, in each rock, in each flower, the earth teaches us about love, about pain. It shows us that passion is not only of the heart, but of life itself, in its most beautiful expression.

May this poem be a river, a channel of emotions, that flows through "Deep Roots", without restrictions. May each verse be an embrace, a caress from the earth, and that upon reading it, the reader's soul, awakens and liberates.

### A Song to the Earth (II)

In the dance of the seasons, the earth transforms,
it dresses in a thousand colors, in each leaf that blooms.
Spring brings with it a rebirth of hopes,
where each sprout is a dream, and each flower, a praise.
Summer, with its heat, invites us to passion,
to live with intensity, to love unconditionally.
The earth gives itself to the sun, in an endless idyll,
and in its warm embrace, teaches us to feel.
Autumn, with its mantle of sunset and melancholy,
reminds us that everything changes, that everything has its day.
The leaves fall, like tears, but not of sadness,
but of gratitude, for life, for nature.
Winter, with its silence, speaks to us of introspection,
of finding in the quiet, our own connection.
The earth rests, but even in its sleep,

it shows us beauty, in the white cloth of ice.
    And so, in each stanza of this poem without end,
    we seek to understand the earth, in its ancestral language.
    It is a song that extends, beyond words,
    it is a feeling that unites us, that is engraved in the soul.
    May "Deep Roots" be a mirror of the heart,
    where each reader can see their passion reflected.

## A Song to the Earth (III)

Because the earth is not just the ground we tread upon,
    it is the home we share, the legacy we leave behind.
    On the canvas of the night, the earth reveals itself,
    a mosaic of shadows, a beauty that consoles.
    The constellations tell tales of ancient loves,
    of gods and mortals, of tragedies and flowers.
    The earth, in its rotation, dances with the stars,
    a destiny waltz woven with threads of alabaster.
    Each mountain, each valley, a verse in its choreography,
    a symphony of forms that challenges the soul.
    The fire of volcanoes, with its fury and might,
    reminds us of indomitable passion, the desire to be reborn.
    The earth, in its ardor, forges and transforms,
    and with each eruption, a new life emerges.
    The sea, with its tides, whispers deep secrets,
    of shipwrecks and treasures, of endless and fertile worlds.

Earth and water, in an eternal embrace,
    speak of a cycle, of ceaseless passage.
    And in the silence of the forest, where time stands still,
    where moss guards the echo of the earth it cradles,
    there, the spirit soars, unencumbered,
    and with every falling leaf, a true story unfolds.
    Thus, this poem unfurls like a rushing river,
    a torrent of emotions, powerful and mysterious.
    "Deep Roots" is a song to what we are,
    to the earth that beckons us, to the dreams we propose.

## A Song to the Earth (IV)

A Song to the Earth (IV)

In the twilight of the gods, the earth still sighs,
with the strength of the seas, with the unwavering light.
It is a song of the ages, an echo of creation,
an ethereal symphony that awakens passion.
The earth, with its valleys and peaks, its endless seas,
is a living poem, a canvas that sketches destiny.
Each creature, each plant, a verse in its song,
united in diversity, in perfect communion.
The thunder in the storm, the calm in the eye of the hurricane,
are the voice of the earth, calling us to contemplate.
It invites us to immerse ourselves in its unparalleled mystery,
to lose and find ourselves in its spiritual abyss.
The earth's passion knows no bounds or age,
it is the force that moves mountains, that gives life to the city.


It is unconditional love, sacrifice, and devotion,
the earth is poetry that floods the soul.
And so, this poem becomes an altar,
where we pay homage to the earth, our home.
"Deep Roots" is a legacy of love,
a gift from the earth that fills us with ardor.

## A Song to the Earth (V)

In the abyss of the night, where secrets are unveiled,
the earth, with its steady pulse, whispers to us.
It is a song that rises from the depths of its being,
a hymn of strength and tenderness that teaches us rebirth.
The earth's passion is an unextinguishable fire,
the eternal flame of life that distinguishes every heart.
It is love that takes root, blossoming in every gesture,
the earth is the stage, and we are its manifesto.
In storm and calm, in joy and sorrow,
the earth embraces us, offering solace.
It is a canvas of emotions, where each color is vital,
where every brushstroke is a step in our astral journey.
And so, this poem unfolds like wings in the wind,
a flight into the unknown, an eternal movement.
"Deep Roots" is a song to what we are,

to the earth that beckons us, to the dreams we propose.
May this book be a reflection, a mirror of the soul,
where each verse is a heartbeat, a caress, a flame.
Because the earth is not just the ground we tread upon,
it is the home we share, the legacy we leave behind.

## A Song to the Earth (VI)

In the embrace of dawn, where the new day awakens,
the earth adorns itself with light, in an open celebration.
It is a song that renews itself with each sunrise,
a promise of life, an eternal rebirth.
The earth's passion is an overflowing river,
that carries strength, that flows constantly.
It is the love that is sown, that germinates in every being,
the earth is the poet, and we are its parchment.
In the vastness of the cosmos, the earth is a bright point, a home of wonders, a vibrant refuge.
It invites us to explore it, to know its depths,
to immerse ourselves in its beauty, in its infinite truths.
The thunder in the storm, the calm in the gentle breeze, are the voice of the earth, etching itself within us. It invites us to feel intensely, to live with fervor,

to love with the strength of the earth, in all its splendor.
And so, this poem becomes an odyssey,
a journey through the earth, an epic.
"Deep Roots" is a song to our essence,
to the earth that inspires us, that graces us with its presence.

## "The Origin of the Elements."

In the beginning, void and nothingness,
a blank canvas awaited creation's touch.
It was the universe's first breath of expansion,
where the elements were born in a grand explosion.
Earth, the foundation, solid and eternal,
with majestic mountains and valleys like cisterns.
She is the base, the home, the origin,
where life takes root, and dreams are woven.
Water, the flow of life, mirror of the sky,
with winding rivers and tranquil seas.
It embodies change, adaptation, and feeling,
in its dance, we reflect and learn to flow.
Fire, divine spark, both destroyer and creator,
its flames consume and provide warmth.
It embodies passion, energy, and power,
in its ardor, we transform and learn to be reborn.
Air, invisible breath, whisper of wings,
with breezes that caress and storms that rage.
It symbolizes freedom, movement, and voice,
in its flight, we ascend and transcend.
Together, these elements weave the fabric of existence,
their interaction condensing life's complexity.
They are the earth beneath our feet,
the water we drink,
the fire within our spirits,
the air we breathe.
In their union, nature's magic unfolds,
a symphony of forces, an unending dance.
Beyond dawn and dusk, in the eternity of space,
the elements shape the cycle, the infinite embrace.
It's a cosmic ballet, a game of power,

where earth, water, fire, and air weave our being.
Earth, with its gravitational force, anchors and defines us,
it's the stage of life, of who we are and who we were.
It holds the past, the present, the future,
the world's memory, its purest countenance.
Water, with its tides and waves, molds and transforms us,
it mirrors our souls, shaping all that exists.
It embodies the flow of time, constant change,
the captivating rhythm of life's course.
Fire, with its heat and light, inspires and renews us,
it is the spark of creation, the one that elevates everything.
It is the fiery passion, the desire, the will,
the energy that drives, the one that can change it all.
Air, with its sigh and song, carries us and guides us,
it is the breath of the spirit, the voice of poetry.
It is the unshackled freedom, the thought that soars,
the inspiration that touches us, the one that makes us stars.
In their union, the elements tell the story of existence,
a tale of creation, survival, and essence.
They are the guardians of balance,
the masters of art,
those who, in their wisdom,
teach us to be a part.
This poem is a tribute to their immortal power,
to the elements that shape us on this astral journey.

## The Origin of the Elements (II)

In the cosmic forge, where stars are born, the elements intertwine in stories that shimmer. It's unbridled passion, an endless desire, nature's masterpiece, both beginning and end.

**Earth**, with its granite body and floral soul, is the cradle of existence, the creator's art. She is the promise of eternity, the refuge of creation, the guardian of secrets, the wellspring of inspiration.

**Water**, with its tears of rain and laughter of waterfalls, is the flowing melody, the long-awaited caress. It mirrors emotions, the canvas of life, the dance of reality, the healer of wounds.

**Fire**, with its dragon breath and sunlit heart, is the transformer, revolutionizing everything. It's the spark of change, the warmth of love, the purifier of souls, the bearer of ardor.

**Air**, with its stormy voice and gentle sigh, is the messenger of dreams, the force that improvises. It expands the spirit, invites freedom, the conductor of adventure, the infinite truth.

In their cosmic embrace, the elements narrate the odyssey, a tale of passions, struggles, and battles.

They are the protagonists of the ancient story, dancing infinitely, shaping life.

## The Origin of the Elements (III)

In the silence of the cosmos, where darkness is illuminated, the elements whisper in a divine symphony. It's a song that transcends, breaking the veil of forgetfulness, an ancestral melody woven into the infinite fabric.

**Earth**, with its mantle of life, its pulse of seeds, is the nurturing mother, cradling us in her wondrous arms. She promises tangibility, the touch of the divine, the sculptor of landscapes, the most genuine love.

**Water**, with its flow of mysteries, its embrace of oceans, is the source of the sacred, the arcane rituals. It embodies intuition, the depth of the soul, the healer of wounds, calming all in its path.

**Fire**, with its indomitable spirit, its stellar dance, is the architect of destiny, forging footprints. It is the flame of inspiration, the kiss of transformation, the guardian of thresholds, the bearer of vision.

**Air**, with its horizon caress, its breath of freedom, weaves dreams, creates clarity. It speaks of the ethereal, the sigh of creation, the messenger of change, the breath of innovation.

In their celestial concert, the elements narrate an epic, a tale of alchemy, passions, and odyssey. They are the architects of being, the poets of the universe, forever revealing verses in their eternal song.

## The Origin of the Elements (IV)

In the heartbeat of the universe, where galaxies intersect, the elements dance in an unending passion. It's a vibrant song that pierces the soul of the cosmos, a melody that unites us, making each note colossal.

**Earth**, with its embrace of roots, its kiss of mud, is the essence of reality, both end and refuge. She embodies constancy, patience, and depth, the mother who teaches us, revealing truth.

**Water**, with its rain caress and oceanic embrace, is the transparency of being, ceaselessly flowing. It reflects the sky, purity, and emotion, molding us gently, granting us a song.

**Fire**, with its comet-like fervor and hearth's warmth, is the spark of existence, the desire to fight. It purifies with force, capable of transformation, bestowing passion and teaching us love.

**Air**, with its eagle's flight and gentle breeze, elevates us with freedom, always signaling. It

brings inspiration, touches everything, leading us to dream, guiding us to the summit.

In their cosmic symphony, the elements narrate an adventure, a tale that stirs emotions, capturing every being. They are the heroes of our story, igniting our spirits, in their infinite dance, teaching us to soar.

### The Origin of the Elements (V)

In the whisper of the wind, where legends rise, the elements sing in harmonies that embrace us. It's a song of unity resonating in our hearts, a melody that envelops us, filling us all.

**Earth**, with its dance of seasons, its endless cycle, is the living history, the stage of divine destiny. She embodies the patience of centuries, the wisdom of the soil, the nurturing mother who provides solace.

**Water**, with its life cycle and eternal renewal, is the source of purity, the essence of creation. It is the healing balm, the channel that guides us, revealing truth through its transparency.

**Fire**, with its fervor for life, its touch of light, is the soul of change, an inexhaustible force. It propels our passion, unites us with warmth, eliminating darkness in its radiant glow.

**Air**, with its freedom from the skies, its deep breath, is the dream of heights, boundless flight. It ascends as inspiration, a voice that elevates us, offering peace in its ethereal embrace.

### The Origin of the Elements (VI)

In the stillness of the ether, where worlds are forged, the elements whisper secrets in a language that transcends. It's a song of connections resonating in the spirit, a melody of existence that fills us all.

**Earth**, with its ancestral pulse, its essence of home, is the refuge of dreams, where everything can begin. She embodies the strength of life, the pillar of being, the nurturing mother who cradles us, allowing us to grow in her embrace.

**Water**, with its sacred flow, its dance of currents, is the mirror of the sky, its depths shining bright. It is the balm for the soul, the river of truth, guiding us to the essence along its clear course.

**Fire**, with its passionate ardor, its eternal radiance, is the heart of change, the architect of love. It's the force that transforms, perpetually renewing, propelling us forward in its unwavering flame.

**Air**, with its breath of life, its whisper of freedom, carries dreams within its boundless expanse. It speaks of hope, guides us like the wind, and challenges us to soar high on its breeze.

In their infinite embrace, the elements narrate passion, a tale that intoxicates us, inspiring creativity. They are the cosmic masters, making us feel alive, teaching us to dance divinely, to truly live.

*In these pages lie the imprints of my soul,*
*traces that breathe life into Gaia's essence.*
*Each image, a whisper from the earth,*
*a song to fire, air, and water.*
*Here, nature's passion overflows,*
*colors dancing beneath the sun's gaze,*
*shadows murmuring secrets at twilight,*
*each line telling the tale of eternal love.*
*Let your heart wander amidst these creations,*
*let each element speak to you, touch you, transform you.*
*They are more than mere images; they are life, they are dreams,*
*the silent voice of the world that surrounds us.*

### The Dance of the Seasons:

Spring: Rebirth in Green

Beneath winter's cloak, life lay in silent anticipation, awaiting spring's sweet kiss, the joyous revelation. With its arrival, the world awakens, trembles, in a rebirth of colors, where everything blossoms.

Tender shoots emerge, the earth dons its finest attire, each flower a note in the symphony that never tires. A time of promises, of fresh beginnings, where hope weaves bonds of immense feelings.

Spring is a spiritual chant, a prayer for life, a passionate whisper inviting creation's strife. In its dance, it beckons us to join the eternal cycle, to celebrate life in its tenderest sanctuary.

As the sun caresses the earth with fingers of light, spring unfurls its mantle—a seductive sight. It's the season of awakening, love in full splendor, where each bud pulses, a creator's tender render.

Fields adorn themselves in vibrant, pure green, each petal unfurling—a miracle, a future unseen. Spring is a living poem, an overflowing passion, a rebirth of life, a heartbeat in rapid succession.

The fragrance of flowers ascends—an organic incense, an offering to life, a spiritual recompense. A time of unity, nature in sacred communion, where earth and sky merge in harmonious union.

Spring invites us to be reborn with it, to bloom, to leave behind the cold past, embrace life's room. It calls us to feel intensely, to live with fervor, to love with the earth's strength, in all its grandeur.

Spring whispers renewal and hope in every corner, a dance advancing across the earth's vast border. It's life's awakening, a canvas painted anew, a season of infinite beauty bestowed by nature.

Gardens resound with melodies, birds sing in chorus, celebrating the returning warmth, a world transformed. Spring is a love poem, a passion unbridled, a symphony of life that bursts forth, undefiled.

Spring: Rebirth in Green

Beneath winter's cloak, life lay in silent anticipation, awaiting spring's sweet kiss, the joyous revelation. With its arrival, the world awakens, trembles, in a rebirth of colors, where everything blossoms.

Tender shoots emerge, the earth dons its finest attire, each flower a note in the symphony that never tires. A time of promises, of fresh beginnings, where hope weaves bonds of immense feelings.

Spring is a spiritual chant, a prayer for life, a passionate whisper inviting creation's strife. In its dance, it beckons us to join the eternal cycle, to celebrate life in its tenderest sanctuary.

As the sun caresses the earth with fingers of light, spring unfurls its mantle—a seductive sight. It's the season of awakening, love in full splendor, where each bud pulses, a creator's tender render.

Fields adorn themselves in vibrant, pure green, each petal unfurling—a miracle, a future unseen. Spring is a living poem, an overflowing passion, a rebirth of life, a heartbeat in rapid succession.

The fragrance of flowers ascends—an organic incense, an offering to life, a spiritual recompense. A time of unity, nature in sacred communion, where earth and sky merge in harmonious union.

Spring invites us to be reborn with it, to bloom, to leave behind the cold past, embrace life's room. It calls us to feel intensely, to live with fervor, to love with the earth's strength, in all its grandeur.

Spring whispers renewal and hope in every corner, a dance advancing across the earth's vast border. It's life's awakening, a canvas painted anew, a season of infinite beauty bestowed by nature.

Gardens resound with melodies, birds sing in chorus, celebrating the returning warmth, a world transformed. Spring is a love poem, a passion unbridled, a symphony of life that bursts forth, undefiled.

Amidst the scorching solstice, we find you, summer of unbridled passions, where long days become anthems, and nights, in dreams, sprout wings.

Your warmth, like a divine breath, awakens life in every seed, and as the world spins, a delicate destiny, you dance as a mesmerizing fire.

Lovers seek each other beneath your sky, a play of glances and tender touches, and with each encounter, a fresh longing, a desire born pure and precise.

You are the season of transformation, in your embrace, the earth renews, and the human spirit takes shape, seeking a newer light.

Oh summer, your essence intoxicates us, in every wave, every grain of sand, and within your forge's depths, passion is forged—eternal and complete.

May your dance carry us, elevate us, to grasp life in its fullness, and with each daring heartbeat, find the highest gratitude.

Summer: The Passion of the Zenith

At the zenith of boundless skies, where the sun reigns with fiery might, winds are unshackled, and destinies unfold, in a summer that feels almost like a plea.

**The earth**, thirsty, trembles, under the weight of an all-encompassing heat, and in its bosom, the seed that blooms, is witness to a fiery ambush.

Summer: The Awakening of Passion

At the zenith of time, eternal summer, where every second pulses with life, a curtain of modern mysteries unfolds, and existence itself feels ignited.

Heat envelops us, seizes us, carries us, in a waltz of emotions that never rests, and at the heart of the fire that tests all, a feeling is born, reveling in everything.

It's summer, the forge of destinies, where each moment becomes sacred, and souls find themselves on divine paths, embraced by ever-illuminated light.

Hearts beat to the rhythm of the day, and at night, a concert of dancing stars, each twinkle a new melody, a universe of vibrant dreams.

Oh summer, your passion inspires us, to seek life's fullest expression, and within the sun's dance, a spinning flame, igniting in us the purest passion.

May your strength guide us, shape us, elevate us, in the ardent pursuit of love without end, and with each whisper carried by the wind, may we discover the echo of celestial longing.

Summer: The Awakening of Passion

In the fullness of summer, life cries out, with a whisper of waves caressing the shore, and in every grain of sand, a flame,

Summer: Tears of the Sun

In the stillness of summer, the world falls silent, before the majesty of a sun that declines, and with each sunset, a palette explodes, in a farewell that both moves and fascinates.

The day's heat turns into a gentle caress, while the earth sighs into rest, and in every blade of grass, a profound dream, inviting us to feel, pure and joyful.

It's summer, with its light spilling forth, an ocean of immeasurable time, where each life ignites, flame by flame, in an endless cycle, the essence of existence.

The stars, in their silent dance, remind us of the fleeting nature of the moment, and with each twinkle, a precious truth, binding us to the universe, unwaveringly.

Oh summer, your splendor overwhelms us, embracing life in its entirety, and within the depths of your gaze, the soul awakens, feels, and arcs, may we discover the truth always hidden.

Summer: The Whisper of Twilight

When twilight kisses the horizon, and summer dresses in its farewell finery, a whisper of time pauses at the fountain, and life is painted in hues of existence.

The day's heat transforms into a gentle embrace, and the sky adorns itself with early stars, each one recounting stories of steps taken, of loves and dreams on early nights.

It's summer, with its endless cycle, where each ending becomes a fresh beginning, and in its

farewell, an unbounded feeling, leading us to dream beyond mere reverie.

The sun's passion now softens, in a play of lights that dusk brings, and in that moment, the soul expands, with the promise of a dawn already born.

Oh summer, your legacy is eternal, in the memory of earth and sky, and within the warmth of your tenderness, the secret of sincere love lies concealed.

May your nights continue to tell us stories, of life's dance and its glories, and with each twilight, may emotion, flood us, like your sun, with devotion.

Summer: The Breath of Evening

As the sun plunges into the abyss, and summer whispers its final verse, the sky adorns itself with a prism, colors that paint the universe.

The nocturnal breeze, bearer of dreams,


Summer: The Whisper of Twilight

When twilight kisses the horizon, and summer dresses in its farewell finery, a whisper of time pauses at the fountain, and life is painted in hues of existence.

The day's heat transforms into a gentle embrace, and the sky adorns itself with early stars, each one recounting stories of steps taken, of loves and dreams on early nights.

It's summer, with its endless cycle, where each ending becomes a fresh beginning, and in its farewell, an unbounded feeling, leading us to dream beyond mere reverie.

The sun's passion now softens, in a play of lights that dusk brings, and in that moment, the soul expands, with the promise of a dawn already born.

Oh summer, your legacy is eternal, in the memory of earth and sky, and within the warmth of your tenderness, the secret of sincere love lies concealed.

May your nights continue to tell us stories, of life's dance and its glories, and with each twilight, may emotion, flood us, like your sun, with devotion.

Autumn: The Melody of Change

When autumn arrives, the wind whispers, with leaves dancing in a golden waltz, and with each descent, a slow movement, speaking of renewed times.

The forest dons ochres and yellows, a spectacle of vibrant nature, and in the rustling of branches, the simple, secrets of life that always inspire.

It's autumn, the painter of landscapes, with brushstrokes of calm and reflection, and on its canvas, the fruits of journeys, from a sun that hides, with gratitude and passion.

Fields prepare for rest, after a long dance of abundance and toil, and in their repose, a warm haven, of stories told with love.

Oh autumn, your arrival inspires us, to find beauty in change, and within the depths of your departure, the promise of a cycle beginning anew.

May your days teach us patience, to await the harvest that will come, and in each fallen leaf, the knowledge, that everything changes, and that's okay.

## Autumn: The Sigh of Memory

In the silence of autumn, memory whispers, with leaves falling like tears of time, and in each one, a story murmurs, of lost loves, sweet lament.

The forest becomes a cathedral of thoughts, where each trunk is a pillar of history, and in the tapestry of leaves, feelings, interlace in a mosaic of victory and defeat.

It's autumn, guardian of memories, with its mantle embracing serenity, and in its freshness, the sincerest dreams, of a departing warmth, gentle and complete.

Fields rest in peace, awaiting a new cycle that will bring life, and in their stillness, a sincere promise, that after the fall, there is a rise.

## Autumn: The Heart of the Earth

In the heart of autumn, the earth sings, with a chorus of leaves surrendering to the wind, and in each melody, a captivating hope, of cycles ending and life freely given.

The forest adorns itself in a mantle of silence, where every step echoes into eternity, and in the whisper of time, a reverent council, inviting us to listen with serene intent.

It's autumn, sculptor of days, with its chisel carving into the human soul, and within its work, the imprints of melodies, from a universe that, in its wisdom, unites us.

Rivers murmur tales of yore, their waters reflecting a softer sun, and in their flow, a tranquil disillusion, teaching us that everything flows, everything continues.

Oh autumn, your palette of emotions unveils, an ever-defining spectacle of colors, and within the depths of your consoling nature, lies the passion of life that aligns us.

May your twilights gift us with beauty, as each day closes with promises of return, and with every falling leaf, the certainty, that beyond sunset, there will always be a new horizon.

Autumn: The Echo of Feelings
In the stillness of autumn, the soul listens, to the echo of feelings resonating, and in each leaf that descends to the ground, a life story unfolds.

The forest dons a passionate red, in a farewell that burns like a slow fire, and in the air, an aroma of renewal, inviting us to introspective encounters.

It's autumn, a comforting embrace, in the murmur of time growing shorter, and within its palette, the promise of a door, open to reflection, perpetually available.

### Autumn: The Whisper of Twilight

In the twilight of autumn, the voice of time, rises in a song of farewell and gratitude, and with each falling leaf, a slow descent, speaking of endings, change, and stillness.

The forest sheds its vibrant green splendor, an act of surrender, unparalleled beauty, and in the tapestry it weaves, a warm hue, enveloping us in a natural embrace.

It's autumn, with its ancestral wisdom, teaching us that everything has its moment, and in its transformation, a vital cycle, reminding us that life is perpetual motion.

Ripe fruits fall, embraced by the earth, a gesture of love, a cycle completing, and within that acceptance lies a lesson, the importance of letting go, returning to the soil.

### Autumn: The Legacy of Time

In the twilight of autumn, the legacy of time, unfolds in a mantle of resting leaves, and in each texture, a memory, a feeling, speaking of stories, of glorious epochs.

The forest dons its gala attire, in a ceremony of colors bidding farewell, and in the air, an advancing chill, preparing us for winter, for frost.

It's autumn, with its slow and sweet decline, reminding us that life is a perpetual spin, and in its farewell, a beauty to be honored, teaching us to value, to love, to forgive.

Animals prepare for their long slumber, instinct guiding their survival and shelter, and in this readiness, a silent determination, to keep moving forward, to find a companion.

Oh autumn, your wisdom envelops us, in an embrace of dry leaves and promises, and within the depths of your resolution, emotion awakens, candles ignite.

May your chilly mornings stir our souls, to see beauty in transition, in calm, and with each twilight, the passion that embalms,

### Winter: Spiritual Silence

Beneath winter's cold mantle lies, a sacred silence, a pause in time. The earth slumbers, the sky unfolds, a canvas of stars, an eternal whisper.

Bare trees, like monks in prayer, stand tall, in deep meditation. Their branches, fingers reaching skyward, touching life's essence, the unending wheel.

The frigid air, a purifying breath, carries promises of renewal. Each snowflake, a bestowed blessing, a cold kiss, a caress of passion.

Winter, master of cycles, teaches us to release, to let go, to die. To be reborn in spring, with a cleansed soul, in the endless cycle where all emerges anew.

Thus we dance with the seasons, in this divine ballet, where each step is an act of love, an act of faith. Winter invites us to look inward, to find our own light in the darkness.

Passionate Winter:

In the stillness of winter, a fire ignites, in the heart of the earth, in the souls of people. It's the passion that burns, that never surrenders, despite the cold, despite apparent death.

Love grows stronger in extreme cold, like two bodies seeking warmth in an embrace. Winter unites us, makes us cherish the moment, each shared breath, each kiss, each step.

The long night invites introspection, to explore the depths of our being. Winter is a master of reflection, teaching us that even in darkness, we can see.

And so, in the dance of seasons, winter has its place, not as an end, but as a vital part. It reminds us that after passion and frenzy, comes calm, reflection, and a purer, more spiritual love.

Deep Winter:

The night descends, vast and profound, in winter's embrace, its dark cloak. A time for the soul, for seeking, those secrets that remain pure in silence.

Winter: Eternal Silence

Beneath winter's cold mantle lies, a sacred silence, a pause in time. The earth slumbers, the sky unfolds, a canvas of stars, an eternal whisper.

Bare trees, like monks in prayer, stand tall, in deep meditation. Their branches, fingers reaching skyward, touching life's essence, the unending wheel.

The frigid air, a purifying breath, carries promises of renewal. Each snowflake, a bestowed blessing, a cold kiss, a caress of passion.

Winter, master of cycles, teaches us to release, to let go, to die. To be reborn in spring, with a cleansed soul, in the endless cycle where all emerges anew.

Thus we dance with the seasons, in this divine ballet, where each step is an act of love, an act of faith. Winter invites us to look inward, to find our own light in the darkness.

Winter: Reflection

In the silence of winter, truth reveals itself, in each icy breath, in every vigilant star. It's a time for feeling, for allowing the soul to speak, in the stillness of cold, where the spirit stands unyielding.

Winter invites us to plunge into the depths, where thoughts are clear as crystal. It serves as a mirror, undistorted and unfiltered, reflecting the purity of our essence, our core.

In the solitude of the wintry landscape, we find companionship, in the dance of flames, in the crackling of firewood. Winter is a friend who neither judges nor argues, but offers its embrace, its peace that instructs.

And so, in winter, we discover the depth of existence, the beauty in austerity, the wisdom in patience. It's a time for growth, for forging

resilience, and within the heart of cold, finding our own essence.

Winter of the Soul

In the profound winter, a tear slides, down the cheek of the earth, an unspoken confession. It's the weeping of the heavens, the mourning of the breeze, for every fallen leaf, for life slipping away.

The bone-chilling cold also embraces the heart, reminding us of our own fragility. Each snowflake carries a memory, of dreams departed, of promises at rest.

Yet within this wintry lament lies a promise, that life persists, that love endures. For every harsh winter, every trial we face, prepares us for joy, for the embraces we give.

Thus, winter teaches us, with its penetrating cold, that even in sadness, beauty can be discovered.

Winter: Hope

In every tear that falls, in every sigh that breaks, there lies a strength rising, an indomitable spirit.

As winter extends its reach and night refuses to yield, a spark ignites within believing souls. It's hope that glimmers in the biting cold, a beacon in the darkness daring spring to come forth.

The weeping sky transforms into a song, as snow falls like tears shed by saints. It's a joyful weeping for love given, for life persisting through each past winter.

Within the embrace of cold, warmth is found, in memories, in dreams, deep within. Winter is not mere absence; it blooms with presence, promising a tomorrow where love reigns supreme.

And when tears dry, and the soul rises, we know winter is but a part of the balance. For after sorrow and the depth it embraces, comes the joy of rebirth in the eternal dance.


Winter of Renewal:
Beyond the chill numbing souls, the heat of a new awakening brews. Winter, with its frosty mantle and calm, is the crucible where hidden fires reveal themselves.

In every heart beating beneath the ice, a spark awaits its moment to shine. Winter guards the yearning, those dreams spring will soon make real.

It's in the depth of darkest night, that the purest faith kindles its lights. Winter isn't an end; it's a remedy, a gestation time for beauty to mature.

And so, when the sky's tears cease, and the white mantle turns green with hope, we'll recognize that each weighty winter is a prelude to a new dance.

Winter of Memory:

In the silence of winter, **memory stirs**, with recollections flowing like rivers beneath the ice. Each lived moment, every laugh, every tear, becomes an **invaluable jewel**, a glimmer.

The cold reminds us, with its relentless touch, of past stories, of unforgettable loves. It's a time to remember, to feel vulnerable, and in the fragility of being, to discover our tirelessness.

Winter is a canvas, where we paint anew, with colors of nostalgia, brushstrokes of silence. It's the season of the soul, where every thought, turns into a poem, a song to the wind.

And when the snow blankets all we know, we realize that in change, there is renewal. Because every lived winter, every challenge we face, is another chapter in our story, a step toward eternity.

### The Garden of the Night

In the garden of the night, where shadows bloom, whispers awaken from the slumbering earth. The moon, a silver queen, ascends her throne, bathing in her light the daring mystery.

Stars twinkle like fireflies in the sky, weaving constellations, untold stories. Each nocturnal petal, every released fragrance, holds a universe's secret, a sincere passion.

The night wind, bearer of ancient songs, wanders through the dark garden, near whispers and altars. It is the breath of life, revealed in the twilight, a passionate song, a comforting dance.

Beneath the night's cloak, everything becomes possible, dreams take shape, love becomes visible. The garden transforms into a sanctuary of emotions, where each being discovers their depths of passion.

And so, in the stillness of the night, the natural world sighs, with the beauty of the ephemeral, with the inspiring passion. The garden of the night, with its mysteries and enchantment, invites us to explore, to love, to dream, beneath its mantle.

### The Garden of the Night II

In the garden of the night, **passion unfurls**, with every trembling leaf, with every wilting flower. Darkness is a veil that truth does not wear thin, it's the mystery that lives, speaking to us in silence.

The moon, guardian of secrets, of loves and yearnings, illuminates the path for hearts in flight. It's the beacon in the twilight, the guide for desires, in the garden of the night, where everything is more beautiful.

The whisper of the breeze is the song of souls, meeting in darkness, calming in stillness. It's the universe's embrace, the caress that beckons us, to discover in the night the beauty that ensnares us.

And so, in the vastness of this enchanted garden, where life hides and time stands still, we find the essence, immaculate love, in the garden of the night, where everything is sacred.

### The Garden of the Night III

In the garden of the night, where time stands still, nature whispers with a serene voice. Nocturnal flowers unfurl, an act of faith, revealing their essence in the battling darkness.

The moon, confidante of lovers and poets, spills her light upon restless secrets. She's the canvas of passion, the refuge of dreams, where each shadow is a desire, every silence a whispered "I love you."

The cool night air, laden with mysteries, is the breath of the cosmos, the sigh of the ethereal. In the garden of the night, every star is a wish, each breeze an embrace, every moment a longing.

And so, in the intimacy of this enchanted garden, we discover magic, unbridled love. In the garden of the night, where everything is unveiled, beauty and mysteries intertwine eternally.

### The Garden of the Night IV

In the garden of the night, where secrets are kept, life unfolds in a whisper that doesn't delay. Darkness is a cloak that doesn't conceal but shelters, the unfathomable beauty, the passion that doesn't wait.

The moon, with her halo of mystery and elegance, watches the dance of leaves, the eternal waltz. She's the muse of poets, the inspiration for fragrances, which in the garden of the night, are released promptly.

The stars, like notes on a celestial score, compose the universe's melody, an endless song. In the garden of the night, each creature is special, each sound a verse, every moment vital.

The air, infused with the essence of the divine, is the garden's breath, the perfume of destiny. At night, each flower becomes a temple, a path, leading us to explore, to feel, to be pilgrims.

And so, in the vastness of this nocturnal garden, we discover the infinite, eternal love. In the garden of the night, where everything is pure, beauty and mysteries embrace securely.

### The Garden of the Night V

In the garden of the night, where secrets intertwine, darkness dons a silence that embraces. It is the sanctuary of the unknowable, the altar of the immense, where the soul submerges, and the heart intensifies.

The moon, with her light of hope and mystery, guards the gates of the ethereal emporium. In her reflection, we find lost paths, hidden desires, and dreams unfulfilled.

The stars, sentinels of vastness, guide us through eternity. In the garden of the night, each light is a message, a whisper from the past, a harbinger of the journey.

The wind, with its melody of ancient legends, carries the stories entrusted by time. It is the night's narrator, the bearer of truth, unfurling majestically in the garden.

### The Garden of the Night VI

In the garden of the night, where whispers become songs, shadows dance to the rhythm of a directionless wind. It is the stage of the unexplored, the domain of imagination, where each nocturnal flower is a stanza of an ancient prayer.

The moon, with her serene glow, is the mistress of ceremonies, directing the spectacle of lights and shadows, of tales and fantasies. She is the mirror of the soul, reflecting the deepest desires, in the garden of the night, where dreams become absolute.

The stars, as guides to destinies and fates, invite us to follow their paths, to unravel their enigmas and debates. In the garden of the night, each twinkle is a promise, a pathway to the unknown, a nature expressing itself.

The air, laden with the fragrance of the unfamiliar, is the perfume of mystery, of feelings uncontained. At night, each aroma is a verse, every breeze a poem, leading us to discover, in darkness, life's diadem.

### The Garden of the Night VII

In the garden of the night, where the moon weeps, her silver tears treasured by the earth. It is the weeping of beauty, the enamoring pain, in the stillness of shadows, where feelings emerge.

The moon, with her pale light, caresses the flowers, that open in darkness, revealing their hues. It's a silent spectacle, a parade of loves, where each petal is a dream, each scent an honor.

The stars, witnesses to this solemn act, twinkle gently in the sky that fears us. In the garden of the night, each twinkle is an emblem, of renewed life, of redeemed love.

The air, bearer of the garden's secrets, is the messenger of passion, of beginnings and endings. At night, each breeze is a sigh, a feast, inviting us to feel, to live, to be jasmine.

And so, in the vastness of this nocturnal garden, we discover beauty, eternal love. In the garden of the night, where everything is pure, beauty and mysteries embrace securely.

### The Garden of the Night VIII

In the garden of the night, where echoes resonate, the souls of lovers secretly converge. It is the corner of the universe where passions run wild, where each heartbeat is a verse, every sigh a chain.

The moon, with her melancholic light, bathes every corner, revealing hidden beauty, the depth of the heart. She is the accomplice of secrets, the refuge of passion, in the garden of the night, where emotions unfurl.

The stars, witnesses to immortal love, illuminate the pathways in this celestial dance. In the garden of the night, each twinkle is a portal, inviting us to dream, to love, beyond the threshold.

The air, infused with an ancestral whisper, is the thread connecting past and present. At night, each aroma is a memory, a ritual, leading us to explore the essence of good and evil.

And so, in the vastness of this nocturnal garden, we discover beauty, eternal love. In the garden of the night, where everything is pure, beauty and mysteries embrace securely.

## Pause on the Path of Verses

## In the Path of Poetry

*In the path of poetry, we pause for a moment, to breathe in the beauty that pulses vibrantly in each verse.*

*It's a time for reflection, to feel the heartbeat, of the words we've shared, of uncontained art.*

*Here, amidst chapters of dreams and metaphors, we take a pause to thank the hours. For every emotion they've allowed us to explore, for every tear, every laugh, every desire to soar.*

*This page is a threshold, a door between worlds, where past and future converge in a second. It's a space to honor the journey we've embarked upon, to embrace the mystery of what lies ahead, the unknown.*

*So take this moment, dear reader, just for you, immerse your soul in silence, listen closely. The whisper of inspiration, the muse's call, invites you to continue, to discover, in poetry, the light that guides.*

*Soon, the pages will turn again, the journey will resume, with new poems that will lift heart and spirit. But for now, rest in this pause, in this stillness, and prepare for what awaits, with renewed gratitude.*

*The next chapter awaits, promising inspiration, with verses that will be beacons in the night of imagination.*

### Scars of the Earth I

In the whisper of the wind, I hear lamentations, of fallen trees, trapped in time, torn roots, leaves carried by the breeze, stories of once-vibrant green now dimmed.

The mountains weep stones of sorrow, their snow-capped peaks shedding tears like glaciers, the echo of their grievances a resounding plea, for every mark we've left in our passing.

The vast and profound seas churn, each wave narrating tales of affliction, bleached corals, fish struggling, in murky waters, seeking redemption.

The sky, once a canvas of blues and oranges, now tainted by the smoke of our ambition, each breath of progress a stain, in the once-pure air turned oppressive.

And we, the architects of this transformation, gaze upon the scars we've etched, hoping somehow to heal the wounds, the Earth we've wounded.

May this poem serve as a reflection, a warning, to care for our home with love and respect, for every action leaves a trace, a spell,

### Scars of the Earth VIII

In the book of life, our most precious secret, beneath the moon, the earth sighs, carrying open wounds upon its chest, each furrow a story that inspires, to remember what silently awakens.

The rivers, veins of life flowing, now bear the weight of our greed, their clear waters, once diluting all, cry out for a future free from malice.

The fire that burns, not only in logs, but also in the souls of ancient forests, reminds us that nature dreams, of being more than an echo of our follies.

The fauna, mirror of our existence, reflects fear and pain in its eyes, against the shadow of our persistence, in marking the world with our errors.

Yet even in the deepest wounds, lies the seed of a new beginning, where our hands, no longer blunt, can caress instead of harm.

May each scar guide us on the path, to a future where compassion reigns, where humanity is no longer its own fate, but the guardian of its own creation.

On the horizon, where sky meets sea, the dawn brings promises of a new day, where every being can, without burden, live in harmony, free from melancholy.

Deserts, with their sand and solitude, teach us the strength of persistence, despite drought, there is vitality, a reminder of our own existence.

The wind carries seeds of hope, crossing valleys, mountains, and plains, breathing life into the earth, still teetering, on the edge of existence, with its sweet remedies.

The night, adorned with a mantle of stars, reminds us we are not alone, each light a dream taking flight, a desire to unite, without suspicion.

And so, the scars of the Earth transform, into life lessons, love, and resilience, a call to action, to be different, to leave a trail of light in our existence.

### Scars of the Earth (Part II)

With each dawn, the Earth implores, through dew-kissed petals of the purest flower, a call to consciousness that doesn't delay, to witness the enduring beauty within her.

The oceans, with their tides and secrets, hold deep within their depths a lament, for the creatures hidden in their recesses, suffering from a changing home's torment.

The air, bearer of life and dreams, is invaded by a gray veil, a reminder of our endeavors, which sometimes forget what it means to truly live.

The Earth, with her infinite patience, awaits our learning from the past, each mistake, each wound that afflicts, guiding us toward a more mindful future.

May these scars not merely be memories, of our missteps and wrongdoings, but maps leading to a new narrative, where healing and hope intertwine.

### Scars of the Earth (Part II)

With each word, each verse, we seek to touch the reader's soul, so that, upon closing this universal book, they feel the call to be a protector.

The Earth spins, silent and strong, in its eternal dance around the sun, yet it bears on its skin the stigma of death, of species fading away without farewell.

The glaciers, witnesses of time, vanish like tears in the sea, a frozen lament, a slow dirge, for the heat of our unyielding indifference.

The jungles, lungs of the world, breathe with difficulty under siege, each fallen tree a second, escaping a future without remedy.

But even in the darkest night, the light of hope shines faint and clear, the possibility of a cure, for the wounds our greedy presence inflicts.

Hands joined, hearts in harmony, we can be artisans of repair, weaving each day with love, a tapestry of life, diversity, unity.

May these scars not be endings, but beginnings of a more conscious era, where the imprints we leave are signals, of respect and love for this living home.

The firmament tells silent stories, of constellations watching from above, witnesses to a world in imbalance, still seeking ways to heal the wound.

Deserts, with their vastness and mystery, speak of resilience, of survival, in sands that have witnessed the empire, of man over the earth, without restraint.

The fauna, in its infinite diversity, faces an uncertain future, yet teaches us that life pulses, in every open and caring gesture.

And so, the scars we leave behind, are not merely evidence of our existence, but calls to awaken, to love, this planet that implores our patience.

May each step we take upon the earth, be light, with respect and consideration, and may we remember that our own battle, should not be against the home that grants us creation.

In the silence of the night, the Earth meditates, pondering the wounds that time cannot erase, each crack a tale that cries out, the urgency of a change no longer delayed.

The poles, with their brittle ice, whisper farewell to the white giants, a mirror of the future, a warning, of days to come if we remain distant.

The stars, witnesses of eons, blink with a light of concern, for a world forgetting its lessons, consumed by its own creation.

Earth, our mother and refuge, extends her arms in a gesture of love, despite pain, despite bitter burdens, she offers forgiveness without resentment.

And with each dawn, a promise emerges, that we can still heal the wounds, that through acts of kindness, piece by piece, we can rebuild lives anew.

May the tears we shed for her, be seeds for a kinder future, where humanity, in its brilliance, finds peace and a stable path.

### Scars of the Earth (Part III)

When the sun sets, and the night embraces, the Earth dons a star-studded cloak, each light a whisper from the vast terrace, where the universe contemplates, marveling.

The rivers murmur lullabies, to the creatures resting on their banks, a watery cradle beneath the moon, promising a tomorrow where life advances.

The meadows, with their infinite green, sway to the rhythm of a gentle breeze, a canvas of peace, devoid of outcry, where each flower and blade of grass holds love.

And in the latent heart of the Earth, beats the pulse of insistent life, a constant and present reminder, that there is still time if humanity persists.

May these scars transform into art, into stories of change, valor, and determination, where every human takes part, in the healing of this dream.

In the stillness of dawn, the Earth renews, with dew caressing each leaf and flower, a daily rebirth, a lesson that uplifts, the hope for change, for a better world.

The fields, with their crops and fruits, remind us of nature's generosity, a life cycle that, despite sorrows, offers sustenance, beauty, and strength.

The sky, after the storm, clears, revealing a deep and serene blue, a canvas of possibilities reflecting, the promise of complete balance.

And in the beating of every human heart, echoes the Earth's call to us, to be custodians of this treasure so early, to honor life, with every word, every drama.

May these scars not merely be footprints of the past, but signs of learning, of evolution, where each step we take, each path we tread, leads us toward the light, toward restoration.

Thus, with every verse that springs from the soul, we hope the reader feels inspired, to be part of the cure, to join the calm, and to care for this home, our beloved legacy.

As twilight descends upon the days, the Earth whispers, with the voice of a thousand rivers, mountains, and seas, a song of life that murmurs in the soul, the story of a home that burns amidst tears.

The ancient forests, with their wisdom, tell of times when harmony reigned, where humans and nature, in symbiosis, crafted together a world without abyss.

Rain falls like tears from the sky, purifying the air, the earth, the veil, which covers our eyes, clouds our vision, of a possible future, brimming with passion.

And in each drop, a reflection of hope, that we can still change our dance, that every step, every choice, can be the beginning of a new song.

May the scars we've left behind, serve as reminders of a past, we do not wish to repeat or relive, but rather transform into a reason to unite.

Thus, with every verse I spill upon this paper, I hope the reader feels the longing, to be part of the change, to be the one, who, with love, heals the wounds of this soil.

## Symphony of Fauna

In the concert of life, each creature, an instrument, a voice in nature, a symphony that endures within the fauna, celebrating life with pure beauty.

The lion roars in the savanna, powerful, its melodic roar an ancestral call, the eagle in the sky, majestic, its song an echo of unparalleled freedom.

Dolphins dance in deep blue seas, their whistles notes in an oceanic score, the butterfly, with its wings, paints the world, in a flight that is poetry, arcane music.

The wolf howls beneath the full moon, a ballad of the pack, of connection, the hummingbird, in its dance, barely pauses, a rapid vibrato from flower to flower, a song.

Every being, from the elephant to the insect, from the whale to the reef fish, plays its part in this perfect act, linking its existence with that of the earth, its relief.

Thus, the world's fauna intones its anthem, a song of diversity, unity, and life, reminding us that each animal, each destiny, is a vital note in the promised land.

### Symphony of Fauna II

The giraffe, with its neck brushing the sky, strolls among acacias in a silent ballet, its serene gaze a tranquil longing, for a world where life is ever present.

The sparrow, in its flight, paints brushstrokes, on the canvas of air with vibrant trills, a modest symphony at daybreak, reminding us of the beauty in constancy.

The fish, in their coral-purple abode, weave harmonies in the dancing water, a spectacle of colors, an imprint, of life flowing tirelessly and vibrantly.

The bear, as it steps, exudes inspiring strength, each footprint resonating a deep note, in the forest, its home, where life revolves, within a cycle of dreams where everything is worthwhile.

Thus, every animal, from the largest to the smallest, from the majestic eagle to the humble snail, gifts us a melody, a dream, a song to life that fills us with sunlight.

May this symphony of fauna lead us, to value each species, each existence, to protect the daring diversity, and be the music of our conscience.

### Symphony of Fauna III

In the embrace of the earth, each animal, a narrator of the oldest tale, sings with a voice that is natural, a hymn to life that intrigues the soul.

The tiger, in the jungle, walks with mystery, its presence a poem of strength and respect, the whale, in the ocean, a solemn sigh, a deep song resonating in the chest.

Monkeys, in the trees, play and dance, a choreography of freedom and joy, their laughter a reminder that they still reach, to touch our souls, filling us with energy.

The elephant, wise and gentle giant, trunks raised to the sky, intones a prayer, a verse of memory from a vibrant past, teaching us the value of conservation.

And so, each creature, with its unique song, invites us to listen, to feel, to understand, that the symphony of fauna is a lesson, of coexistence, of love we must ignite.

## Symphony of Fauna IV

In the silence of the forest, a whisper is heard, the voice of the Earth singing to her children, each animal a verse, a murmur, weaving its brilliance into life's tapestry.

The deer, in the mist, walks like a phantom, its ethereal form a ballet in the haze, a gentle reminder of nature's vastness, enveloping us in its mantle, uniting us.

Birds, in their flight, trace melodies, notes ascending, touching the sky, a winged choir that dissolves in the air, filling us with pure and sincere emotion.

The fox, with its cunning, roams the path, its tail a brush painting the night, a free spirit, a nimble wanderer, teaching us that life is an extravagance.

And in every animal's gaze, a reflection, of the beauty inherent in living, in being, a call to care, with every gesture, for the symphony of fauna, our duty.

## Symphony of Fauna V

In the breath of the earth, every beast and bird, a sigh of creation, a divine song, a melody etched into the soul, like a sacred mantra, a pilgrim's destiny.

The jaguar, spirit of the humid jungle, moves like a shadow, a mystery gliding, its gaze a window to a world entrusted, to ancestral wisdom, eternally inscribed.

Bees, in their labor, hymn the work, pollinating life in a sacred flight, each visited flower a pact, an embrace, within nature's golden temple.

The horse, with its gallop, pulses rhythm, across vast prairies, a liberated spirit, an echo of freedom carried on the wind, inviting us to run, to dream, boundless.

And so, each creature, with its light and shadow, teaches us that life is a spiritual canvas, where every brushstroke, every form, astounds, uniting us in a cosmic dance, a ritual.

### Symphony of Fauna VI

In the breath of the earth, every beast and bird, a sigh of creation, a divine song, a melody etched into the soul, like a sacred mantra, a pilgrim's destiny.

The jaguar, spirit of the humid jungle, moves like a shadow, a mystery gliding, its gaze a window to a world entrusted, to ancestral wisdom, eternally inscribed.

Bees, in their labor, hymn the work, pollinating life in a sacred flight, each visited flower a pact, an embrace, within nature's golden temple.

The horse, with its gallop, pulses rhythm, across vast prairies, a liberated spirit, an echo of freedom carried on the wind, inviting us to run, to dream, boundless.

And so, each creature, with its light and shadow, teaches us that life is a spiritual canvas, where every brushstroke, every form, astounds, uniting us in a cosmic dance.

### Symphony of Fauna VII

In each dawn, the fauna awakens, with a chorus celebrating the new day, each song a thread in the certain weave, of life entrusted to Earth.

The owl, in its vigil, observes wisely, guardian of secrets in the starry night, its silent flight a gentle lip glide, speaking to us of a calm, sheltered world.

The frogs, with their croaking, a persistent bass, in the nocturnal concert, a voice that stands out, a rhythm pulsating in the atmosphere, reminding us of the magic that never wanes.

The thrush, with its melody, rouses the forests, a soft prelude heralding the dawn, its trill a golden thread that the orbs, of the sky mimic on their canvas that never fades.

And in each being, from the ant to the bear, from the clownfish to the imperial eagle, a symphony is woven, a beautiful purpose, to coexist in a natural world.

## Portraits of Flora

On Earth's canvas, life sprouts forth, green hope in unfurled leaves, each plant, each tree, a promise fulfilled, of oxygen and dreams, in their uplifted branches.

The trees stand tall, pillars of the sky, with sturdy trunks, roots deep within, guardians of time, bearing a beautiful legacy, whispering stories within each growth ring.

The flowers, with their petals, paint the air, fragrances wafting in a colorful dance, each one a portrait of unwavering nature, a tribute to life's myriad flavors.

The moss, on the stone, a velvet cloak, an artwork in the forest's stillness, it speaks of persistence, of sincere love, growing silently, without the need for fanfare.

And so, every plant, from grass to sequoia, from cactus to vine, reveals beauty, strength, and joy, our companion in the surrounding flora.

May these portraits of flora remind us of the vital importance of every sprouting being, to protect diversity, to be tender, to honor the Earth that sustains us, our host.

In the garden of the spirit, each plant and tree serves as a teacher, a guide on life's path, their leaves, like hands, offering wisdom, peace in the fiery struggle.

The oak, with its strength, teaches resilience, to stand tall in the face of storms, its roots an anchor in existence, a reminder of integrity's significance.

Orchids, delicate in their beauty, speak of fragility and fortitude, the duality of life, of nature, balancing between sorrow and royalty.

The weeping willow, its branches bending, exemplifies humility, the art of empathy, a refuge for the wandering soul, seeking harmony along painful trails.

And thus, every green being, from moss to palm, from violet to majestic cedar, invites us to look beyond mere matter, to feel connected to the whole, to the ether.

May these portraits of flora stir our emotions, lead us to a place of reflection and encounter, where hearts open wide, where eyes peer, at life's beauty, at the love that centers us.

In the whisper of leaves, the voice of flora, a gentle echo carried by the wind, each plant, each tree, a story that blooms, in the garden of the world, a diverse poetry.

The bamboo, in its elegance, speaks of flexibility, the ability to bend but not break, a symbol of resilience, the truth of simplicity, teaching us that in life, adaptation is key.

The sequoias, giants touching the clouds, remind us of beings that live for millennia, witnesses to the passage of time, light, and shadows, standing firm despite the challenges.

The fern, in its ancient greenness, a living fossil, shows us the persistence of life on Earth, a plant that has witnessed the world's changes, and yet continues to grow, untroubled by war.

And so, each member of the flora, in its silence, invites us to listen, learn, and feel, to recognize the wisdom residing in their consensus, in the beauty of existence, in the art of being.

May these portraits of flora lead us to a place of connection with nature, where every leaf, every flower, serves as evidence, of a love for life, of eternal beauty.

In the embrace of Mother Nature, each plant, each tree, a cherished child, gifts us with their breath, their inexhaustible wealth, an act of pure and perfect love.

The cedar and pine, in their solemn height, speak of resilience, of evergreen endurance, a reminder that despite the storms, life clings, rises, and reinvents itself.

Daisies, in their charming simplicity, teach us that beauty resides in the humble, that ostentation is unnecessary for the hour to be filled with magic, with shining moments.

The lily of the valley, its white bell, a gentle hymn to purity, to hope, invites us to believe, to maintain balance, in a world of harmony, free from distrust.

And thus, each being of the flora, in its existence, inspires us to seek, to find the essence, of life pulsating persistently, in an earthly garden brimming with presence.

In Earth's lap, every flower, every leaf, is a sigh, a heartbeat of its heart, a manifestation of love, of crimson joy, that moves us, calls us to reason.

The ancient tree, in its wise stillness, speaks of stories, life cycles, its branches like arms, in an attitude of welcome, of embrace, of farewell.

The veins of its leaves, in vibrant green, trace maps of life, a constant pulse, a reminder that each moment is precious, unique, and significant.

The lotus flower emerges in purity, rising from the mud with elegance, teaching us that beauty can emerge, even in adversity, with hope.

And so, each being of the flora, in its splendor, invites us to feel, to love, to shed tears, for ephemeral beauty, for pain, in a world that forgets how to reverence.

May these portraits of flora move us, not to sadness, but to profound love, for the Earth that endlessly provides, for the life unfolding in this world.

On the canvas of existence, flora paints, with chlorophyll strokes, with life's brushstrokes.

In the whisper of leaves, the voice of flora, a gentle echo carried by the wind, each plant, each tree, a muse that captivates, a symphony of colors on an extended palette.

The olive tree, with its branches, a symbol of peace, offers us its oil, its fruit, its legacy, a testament to times that will never return, of intertwined stories, of a revered past.

Azaleas, ablaze with fire, a burst of passion, remind us that beauty is ephemeral, fleeting, that we must appreciate each moment, each season, with the intensity of those who know everything will fade away.

The cypress, in its height, a beacon pointing, the way to the sky, to the eternal, invites us to lift our gaze, to climb the scale, of spirituality, of sempiternal mystery.

And thus, each being of the flora, in its perfection, inspires us to seek beauty in simplicity, to find greatness in creation, in a world where flora is the temple.

At the dawn of time, flora awakens, with a burst of life received by the dawn, each bud, each flower, an open door, to a world where beauty always thrives.

The magnolia, its flowers like wine goblets, toasts to life in an aroma-filled banquet, its petals a canvas painted by a divine artist, depicting hope in their pristine whiteness.

The vine, in its embrace, extends a hug, speaks of unity, of strength in connection, its clusters a fruit of the earth that seeks only to offer sweetness, without possession.

The poplar, dancing with the wind, its leaves applauding life's symphony, reminds us that each moment is an event, to celebrate existence, so dearly cherished.

And thus, each being of the flora, in its infinite dance, invites us to join, to be part of the spectacle, to feel the emotion of advancing nature, in a spectacular cycle of life.

## Water Chants

In the eternal song of flowing rivers, we hear the voice of murmuring water, stories of Earth cradled in its arms, the pure current of life's cycle.

The seas, with their waves, tell legends, of sailors and creatures in the depths, a sway of mysteries, offerings of nature, symbolizing change and boundless possibilities.

Each drop, a sigh from the heavens, falling gently to kiss the earth, joining rivers on their longing paths, until reaching the sea, their ultimate and sincere destination.

Water, mirror of the world, reflects the moon, and dances with sunlight on its surface, the cradle of life, the source of fortune, teaching us that everything flows, everything is in motion.

### Water Chants (Flow of Existence)

From snow-capped peaks to flower-filled valleys, water meanders, a thread of life embroidering the Earth, in each drop, hidden worlds of secrets, a constant flow descending from the sky.

Streams, with their stone melodies and currents, weave endless concert tunes, each waterfall an applause from the slopes, celebrating a cycle that always finds its end.

The ocean, in its vastness, embraces the world, its tides a deep breath of the Earth, a profound heartbeat, each wave a caress spanning seconds, time slipping away, becoming a wandering vagabond.

Rivers, the geography's arteries, flowing paths, connecting villages, cultures along their banks, witness histories, loves that conclude, lives reflected and unfurled in their waters.

Lakes, mirrors where the sky contemplates itself, hold the calm of a thoughtful world, in their depths, life concentrates, a silence that speaks, sentences to peace.

And thus, every body of water, from puddle to sea, from brook to wide estuary, tells of an eternal quest, the essence of life, its own unique calvary.

### Water Chants (Rivers of Feeling)

Beneath the moon, the river whispers secrets, stories carried from mountain to sea, a journey of stars reflected on its bed, life's path that never ceases to seek.

Water, in its course, embraces the shore, kisses stones, caresses sand, a gentle touch that shines in silence, a melody flowing and filling.

The sea, in its vastness, guards silences, blue depths where time stands still, a universe of corals, fish, reflections, each wave a sigh arriving and departing.

Ponds, tranquil in their peace, harbor souls, mirroring the sky, observing passing clouds, guardians of balance, of calm, where life pauses to contemplate.

And thus, every drop in this aquatic chant, from morning dew to torrential rain, is a verse in the most empathetic poem, of nature a vital song.

### Water Chants (Depths and Heights)

From the depths where the sun cannot reach, to the heights where clouds originate, water ascends and descends in a dance, an endless cycle where forms dignify themselves.

The torrent, in its fury, unbridled power, carves rock, sketches the landscape, a reminder of the unexpected, of life's force, of its free journey.

The calm sea, vast stillness, its deep waters a separate world, each creature, each movement, a virtue, teaching us about life, about art.

Glaciers, in their slow march, sculpt valleys, create crystal rivers, their ice bears witness to time, an altar, where nature displays its cardinal power.

Rainfall, in its descent, a celestial choir, touches the earth with notes of fertility, a water song that gives and takes away, cleansing the world, offering its goodness.

And thus, each element of water, in its essence, from dewdrops to rising tides, is a flowing poem, revealing to us life's ever-changing, eternal struggle.

## Water Chants (Legacy of Flow)

Water, in its journey, knows no borders, crosses continents, unites seas and rivers, a legacy of life awaiting in its flow, to be the bridge between worlds, dreams, and challenges.

Submarine currents, hidden rivers in the sea, carry warmth, carry life in their saline embrace, a silent exchange that never ceases to give, in the depths, a divine destiny.

The spring, at its birth, a source of purity, bubbling from the ground, a miracle sprouting forth, offering clear water with a nature that invites reflection, remote connection.

The swamp, in its stillness, a mirror of the sky, holds life within its calm tension, an ecosystem swaying in flight, as birds glide above it in an intense dance.

And thus, every expression of water, in its essence, from falling rain to melting glacier, is a chant to life, a duty, to care for water, our most exquisite resource.

## Water Chants (Morning Dew and Beyond)

Morning dew, tears of dawn, pearls adorning the face of the earth, messengers of the day unfurling, announcing the sun that cradles life.

The playful brook, liquid laughter, sliding among stones and roots, its melody an idyllic existence, eternally sung by nature.

Mist over the lake, mystical veil, concealing and revealing water's secrets, in its dance, a near-systole ritual, pulsating with the forge's heartbeat.

The fierce storm, wielding its might, unleashes torrents of water, yet after tempest's fury, the river, reemerges stronger, forging its course.

In the endless cycle, water flows, from cloud to sea, sea to sky, each drop carries life's fleeting essence, and in its return, the eternal longing.

Rising mist, the river's sigh, at dawn, a cloak of mystery, the breath of the current, a chill warmed by the sun an imperium.

Breaking ice, winter's finale, in thaw, a promise of renewal, each melting crystal an eternal cycle of life, a dreamlike destiny.

Hot springs, Earth's warmth, a gift welling from its heart, offering clear waters with a nature that invites reflection, remote connection.

The geyser, nature's spectacle, a column of water defying the sky, in its strength, Earth reveals beauty, and as it falls, life multiplies.

Thus, water teaches us through its flow, that everything changes, continues, its movement invites discovery, life's vibrant and constant cycle.

The waterfall whispers, mountain's voice, in descent, a song of freedom, water dancing, never accompanied, on its journey to the sea, it carries truth.

The estuary, water meets salt, where river merges with ocean, a union's chant, a ritual, celebrating life in its arcane flow.

Rising vapor, water's breath, becomes cloud, floats in the sky, an unextinguished cycle, giving life to the earth, ever sprouting.

The glacier, ancient and wise, glides, slow but steadfast on its eternal path, in its ice, history is immortalized, and as it melts, it speaks of winter.

And so, water, in all its forms, is a master of change, life, rhythms, its chants inform us that we are part of its infinite abysses.

The submerged reef, an underwater garden, in its silence, teems with life, corals that have blossomed in water, their colors telling a glorious tale.

## Water Chants (Floods and Beyond)

The flood, unbridled force, sweeps away the old, brings the new, in its fury, the earth is renewed, and in its retreat, leaves the soil refreshed.

The ancient well, profound wisdom, where water rests, serene and wise, connects us to the past, a round of stories dwelling in its depths.

The delta, journey's end, where the river bids farewell, disperses, is an embrace between land and waves, an ending that is a beginning, a reversal.

Rainwater, in its descent, a symphony on rooftops, sings to life, a departure of clouds parting, gifted to the sun.

The puddle, ephemeral mirror, reflects the sky, the city, a reminder, a criterion, of water's presence in its simplicity.

The geyser's bubbling, a prelude, an anticipation of the forthcoming spectacle, a rhythm that repeats, an interlude, in Earth's symphony, a path.

And thus, water, in its constant flow, teaches us about life, its perpetual turning, in each drop, a world to discover, in each wave, a destiny to embrace.

The river on its journey, master of paths, weaves the earth with threads of silver, connecting destinies as it runs, and in its murmur, relaying history.

Rainfall in the forest, a living symphony, note by note, life awakens, each drop received and invigorating the earth, and in its descent, beauty awakens.

Subterranean water, hidden vein, flows silently, life's sustenance, in its journey, the earth thrives, nourished, upheld, in its eternal course.

The tranquil pool, pause in the current, refuge of peace, calm waters, a breath amid constant flow, where life gazes, serene.

The spring that bubbles in the village square, meeting point for stories and laughter, a thread that unites, weaves the fabric of community, in its days and breezes.

The floating ice, witness of cold, sways on the sea, travels in stillness,

The whisper of rain against the window, a gentle melody inviting dreams, it's the song of water that emanates, and in its rhythm, life dances.

The water flowing through the aqueduct, legacy of ancients, Rome's wisdom, in its course, a testament born from engineering and emerging water.

The wave breaking on a distant shore, nature's force, unparalleled might, it's the water that tells, that doesn't deceive, of the sea's strength, of the storm.

The puddle forming after the tempest, reflection of the world on its surface, it's the water that teaches, that nourishes, curiosity, in its simplicity, delight.

The water in the barrel, reserve of life, hope in times of drought, it's the water that helps, that cares, and in its stillness, life trusts.

The frozen river, crystal-clear and calm, in its silence, winter's force, it's the water that pauses, a secret, holding the promise of eternal warmth.

The spring that bubbles from living rock, mountain spring, pure and clear, it's the water that, in its journey, activates, life in its surroundings, in its rarity.

And thus, water, in its eternal wanderings, speaks of cycles, renewal, in its flow, invites us to contemplate, the wonder of life, its song.

The water cascading down the waterfall, a veil of nacre on bare rock, it's the water that sings, that asks for nothing, gives nothing, in its descent, freedom is laid bare.

The brook winding through the meadow, its cool waters tracing a path, it's the water that invites, with its quiet murmur, to follow life's course, in its clear threat.

The water stagnating in the swamp, holds secrets in its somber stillness, it's the water that reflects, year after year, the earth's history, in its melancholy.

The water seeping into the cave, drop by drop, time sculpts and carves, it's the water that dares in darkness, to create hidden beauties, in its silent battle.

The water springing forth in the oasis, in the desert, a miracle, a blessing, it's the water that gives life, that warns of the precious essence of creation.

The water freezing at the pole, in its silence, a world in pause, it's the water that preserves, in its hidden solitude, the planet's memory, in its white cause.

The water evaporating in the tropics, rising invisibly, an endless cycle, it's the water that transforms, in its magical tropics, and returns to the earth as rain, as a garden.

**And thus, water, in its constant flow, teaches us about life, its perpetual turning. In each drop, a world to discover; in each wave, a destiny to embrace.**

**The water that cascades down the waterfall, a nacre veil on bare rock, sings without asking or giving, baring freedom in its descent.**

The brook winding through the meadow, its cool waters tracing a path, invites with its quiet murmur to follow life's course, in its clear threat.

The water stagnating in the swamp guards secrets in its somber stillness, reflecting year after year the earth's history in its melancholy.

The water seeping into the cave, drop by drop, time sculpts and carves, daring in darkness to create hidden beauties in its silent battle.

The water springing forth in the oasis, in the desert, a miracle, a blessing, gives life and warns of the precious essence of creation.

The water freezing at the pole, in its silence, a world in pause, preserves in its hidden solitude the planet's memory, in its white cause.

The water evaporating in the tropics, rising invisibly, an endless cycle, transforms in its magical tropics and returns to the earth as rain, as a garden.

And thus, water, in its eternal wanderings, speaks of cycles, renewal, inviting us to contemplate the wonder of life, its song.

The fierce torrent, in its brave impetuosity, uproots trees, carves stone; it's the water that knows no rest, revered by the earth in its strength.

The water whispering in the brook, tales of fairies, ancient legends; it weaves a tapestry of life, dreams, and deception in its bed.

The water overflowing in the flood, an awakened giant, an ancestral power; it claims dominion over the earth with its mortal dance.

The water calming in the lagoon, a mirror of sky, clouds, and sun; it invites reflection, encounter, and the glow of twilight.

The water vanishing on the horizon, where sky and sea merge; it promises an endless journey where worlds blend.

And thus, water, in its eternal meandering, speaks of cycles, renewal, inviting us to contemplate the marvel of life, its song.

## Water Chants (Short Verses)

# I. The Whisper of the River

The river murmurs in its bed, tales of yore, eternal secrets, in each stone, in each reflection, life flows in tender whispers.

# II. The Dance of the Sea

Waves that dance beneath the moon, passion erupting in white foam, the sea embraces, the sea cradles, in its wild dance, passion unfurls.

# III. The Tear of Rain

Heaven weeping, pure tears, kissing the earth, awakening flowers, life emerges in certain drops, rain sings its myriad loves.

# IV. The Embrace of the Ocean

Deep and vast, blue mystery, the ocean envelops in its grand embrace, currents carry promises of lullabies, within its immense being, everything changes and expands.

# V. The Reflection of the Pond

In tranquil waters, the world gazes, the pond guards silence and calm, on its surface, inspiration blooms, and in its stillness, the soul finds solace.

# VI. The Song of the Brook

Playful and free, the brook flows, joyfully singing among green branches, its melody invites anyone who listens to follow the clear flow of its waters.

# VII. The Journey of the Glacier

Ancient traveler, ice recounting stories of eons in its slow progress, the glacier advances, its deliberate pace teaching that even cold can love.

# VIII. The Hope of the Spring

Source of life, the spring bubbles forth, clear and pure at dawn, a promise of a new day adrift, within its waters, hope can flourish.

# IX. The Mystery of Fog

Veil of mystery, fog extends, over rivers and seas, a gentle embrace, concealing and revealing, its playful dance shows that even in uncertainty, there is meaning.

# X. The Force of the Waterfall

With fervor, the waterfall descends, powerful and untamed in its fierce plunge, its voice resonates, certainty driven home, life's velocity is undeniable.XI. The Swamp's Sigh

Stagnant waters, yet teeming with life, the swamp breathes, a deep sigh, in its stillness, a hidden passion, it guards secrets of the world profound.

# XII. The Ocean's Eternity

Immense and timeless, the ocean awaits, a witness to ages in its salty embrace, each breaking wave tells a sincere story, of water that flows, perpetually renewed.

# I. River of Dreams

In the winding bed of a serpentine river, where dreams flow ceaselessly, each drop pulses with palpable desire, a longing that refuses to rest.

# II. Tides of the Heart

Like tides kissing the shore, love is both eternal and ever-changing, passions distilled by the moon, in nights of fervent ardor.

# III. Ocean of Life

Deep and vast, the ocean proclaims, its waves recounting ancient tales, within its waters, existence spills forth, and laughter and tears remain hidden.

# IV. Tears of Rain

Rain falls, tears from the sky, nourishing the earth with its weeping, each drop a memory, a yearning, germinating enchantment in the soil.

# V. Brook of Hope

There exists a brook where hope, bubbles forth—clear, pure, crystalline, in its course, life balances, like a dance leading toward the future.

# VI. Whispers of the Pond

In the calm of the pond, secrets rest, whispers carried to and fro by the wind, nature's murmurs alight on its surface, reflected in ripples of water.

# VII. Cascade of Emotions

Bravely crashing against bare rock, a waterfall of unbridled emotions, torrents that sparkle in descent, the passion of enamored souls.

# VIII. Spring of Inspiration

From the earth springs the well, a living source of muses and poetry, clear water that enriches verses, trusting inspiration to the ink.

# IX. Summer Rain

Warm rain on a summer afternoon, liquid caresses soothing the heat, each drop a kiss passed from hand to hand, highlighted in the soul's canvas.

# X. Rivers of Time

Rivers flow endlessly toward the sea, bearing stories of bygone eons, within their currents, time navigates, and days are counted along their course.

# Echoes of Humanity

Since the dawn of time, in the cradle of the earth, humanity was born, forged with its essence and its strife. The earth shaped us, gave us form and sustenance, in its valleys and mountains, we found our breath.

With every grain of sand, with every raindrop, we learned to survive in nature's cunning ways. The earth was our teacher; in its lessons, we discovered the strength to rise, and in its embrace, we rested.

We cultivated its fields, sailed its seas, constructed civilizations beneath its starry skies. The earth witnessed our growth, our expansion, our dreams, and in its soil, we left footprints that time won't erase. But we weren't always kind to our mother earth, sometimes we hurt her, causing pain and strife. Yet she forgives, offers us pardon, reminding us that we are one under the same sun.

Echoes of humanity resonate through eternity, we are children of the earth, our truth lies within it. May the echoes of our passage be of love and peace, and may we honor the earth that witnessed our birth and journey.

And so we continue, children of the earth, in our endless voyage, learning and loving with each dawn and dusk. The earth whispers secrets to us in the wind, in the sea, teaching us that every life, every being, is a precious treasure.

In the dance of seasons, in life's cycle, humanity and earth compose a shared symphony. We reap what we sow in this fertile, vast soil, and with every step we take, the earth embraces us.

May the echoes of our existence be filled with respect and gratitude, for the earth that shelters us with its boundless abundance. Let us move forward with hope and faith, honoring the earth, our eternal home, our Eden.

Across the vastness of time, humanity and earth intertwine, an eternal bond, a passion that burns unwaveringly. The earth has seen us born, grow, love, and weep, and in its embrace, we've found solace a place to dream.

With each sunrise, the earth invites us to begin anew, its mountains challenging us to reach for the stars, to soar. Its rivers are like veins, carrying life to every corner, and in the rustle of leaves, we hear its ancient song.

Humanity, with eager hands and passionate hearts, has etched its history into stone, wind, and current. We've learned to dance with the earth, an unending rhythm, a choreography of creation and destruction, of light and shadow, of yin and yang.

The patient earth has taught us to forgive, to understand that we are part of something greater, something to cherish. Our footsteps resonate on its surface, each footprint a promise to live passionately, respectfully, in an unending union.

May the echoes of our passion merge with the earth, our mother, may every act of love pay tribute to its beauty, its purity.

## Echoes of Humanity

Let us forge ahead, with the fire of life in our souls, honoring the earth with every word, every tear, every laugh.

For in the earth, our history is written, our truth, in its forests, its deserts, its oceans, our humanity. May the echoes of our love resonate through eternity, and may earth and humanity remain united, in passion, in freedom.

Thus, at the twilight of time, humanity and earth merge, in an eternal embrace, a promise of an unwavering future. The earth, with its majesty, has witnessed our struggles and triumphs, within its embrace, we've sown dreams that bloom like stars.

Humanity, with its indomitable spirit, has achieved the unimaginable, together, we've penned an unforgettable epic. The earth has given us wings to soar toward infinity, and in each heartbeat of its core, we feel the echo of the infinite.

May the echoes of our existence be a song of hope, a hymn of glory to the earth, which reaches us in its dance. Let us continue onward, with the light of wisdom in our hands, honoring the earth through every action, in all the years to come.

**Because in the earth lies our legacy, our immortal essence, in its seas, its skies, its fire, our vital passion. May the echoes of our love resonate through eternity, and may earth and humanity remain united in majesty.**

**On the horizon of history, where past and future converge, humanity and earth rise together in a vision that grounds us. With each sunrise,**

each sunset, each newborn star, earth and humanity intertwine in a cosmic embrace.

### Echoes of Humanity

### I. Ancestral Whispers

In the earth's silence, ancestral whispers, voices of those who walked before us, in every grain of sand, in millennia-old rocks, the history of humanity forever resonates.

### II. Deep Roots

We are trees with roots plunging deep, absorbing the earth's wisdom, our mother, each ring within us marking a year, a second, in infinite time, our essence, our father.

### III. Chants of Connection

The earth sings, and we echo its melody, in the wind, in the sea, in the river's murmur, our souls intertwine with nature in harmony, and within that song, we find our sacred solace.

### IV. Eternal Footprints

We walk upon the earth, leaving eternal footprints, marking our passage, our history, our being, though time may erase our external steps, the essence of our journey, the earth forever holds.

### V. Temples of Earth

We build temples and altars, reaching toward the sky, yet it is within the heart of the earth that we find the sacred, in its silence, its calm, its eternal solace, we discover the divine, the spiritual, the immaculate.

### VI. Life's Cycles

The earth teaches us life's cycles, of birth and death, in each falling leaf, in every blooming flower, it shows us that all is transient, all transforms, and in that transformation, our souls expand and float.

### VII. Guardians of Legacy

We are guardians of the earth's legacy, its memory, in our hands lies the future of its story, its destiny, with every act of care, respect, and glory, we honor the earth, our home, our path.

### VIII. Echoes of Humanity

And so, the echoes of humanity resonate within the earth, a song of love, hope, and unity, in every mountain, every valley, every cavern, earth and humanity remain together in eternity.

### IX. The Earth's Voice

In the echo of a living, breathing world, we hear the earth's ancient and wise voice, it speaks through falling leaves, murmuring rivers, and the stillness of mountains.

### X. Legacy of Dust

We are children of stardust, of mud and rain, shaped by invisible hands across vast time, each grain of our existence a testament to history, a legacy of the earth, finding its temple within us.

### XI. The Spirit of Stone

In each stone, a spirit that tells a story, of bygone eras, civilizations risen and fallen, the earth is witness and narrator of our glory and memory, and within its embrace, humanity's echoes endure.

### XII. The Song of the Cosmos

The earth, a blue dot in the cosmic chorus, reminds us of our smallness and our grandeur, in its soil, the footprints of our steps, a residue, connecting us to the universe in its beauty.

### XIII. The Dance of Life

We dance upon the earth, a choreography of life and death, with each spin, each step, the earth guides us, and in this dance, we find our compass, our fate, within the earth, our eternal companion.

### XIV. The Sigh of the Wind

The wind carries the sighs of humanity, tales of love, war, peace, and conflict, the earth listens and embraces, in its boundless kindness, the echoes of our lives within its cyclic rhythm.

### XV. The Reflection of Water

In the reflection of water, we see our ever-changing faces, the earth reveals what we were, what we are, what we'll become, in each wave, in every droplet, a vibrant reflection, of humanity living and growing upon the earth.

### XVI. The Inner Fire

The earth burns with an inner fire, a beating heart, and we, with our own fire, seek illumination, within the earth, we find refuge, our struggle, and in its warmth, the passion to live, an impulse, a cross.

### XVII. The Silence of the Stars

We gaze at the night sky, at the silence of the stars, and feel the earth's call, our home, in its mystery, in its silence, in its twinkling, earth and humanity dream together.

**XVIII. The Breath of the Forests**

In the breath of forests, we sense the earth's pulse, a whisper of life hidden among green leaves, it echoes humanity within nature's presence, a bond that unites us, answered by every branch.

**XIX. The Wisdom of the Desert**

The desert, with its eternal dunes, speaks of patience, of vast time, of the silence that teaches, it challenges us, offers resistance, and within its immensity, life's depth is embraced.

**XX. The Mystery of Oceans**

Mysterious and deep, the oceans guard ancient secrets, within their waters, humanity's history is inscribed, the earth calls to us through liquid songs, and in its salty embrace, our existence stirs.

**XXI. The Strength of Mountains**

Majestic and unwavering, mountains speak of fortitude, aspiring to touch the heights, to reach the sky, the earth inspires, offering certainty in its solidity, and atop its summits, our spirit echoes, pure and longing.

**XXII. The Dance of Volcanoes**

Volcanoes, with fire and ash, tell tales of creation and destruction, of the earth's power to give and take life, renewal is their dance of eruption, reminding us that we are part of their wonder.

**XXIII. The Legacy of Glaciers**

Glaciers, with their slow movement, speak of memory, history etched in ice, climates past and future, the earth preserves, guarding stories in its cold, and as they melt, humanity's future unfolds.

**XXIV. The Promise of Dawn**

Each sunrise, with its light and hope, heralds new beginnings, the promise of another day, an opportunity to improve, the earth rejuvenates, granting us dreams in its cycle, and within its radiance, humanity's echoes find color.

**XXV. The Sigh of Dusk**

Every sunset, with its hues and calm, speaks of reflection, the beauty of endings, the peace that accompanies twilight, the earth bids farewell, imparting lessons in its pause, and across its painted sky, humanity's echoes find their place.

### XXVI. The Cave's Echo

In the deep caverns, where echoes linger, our ancestors' footsteps resonate in darkness, the earth guards their secrets, poses questions, revealing life's mysteries, the history we must remember.

### XXVII. The Jungle's Call

The jungle, teeming with life, speaks of abundance, of interconnectedness among all living forms, it vibrates with the call to be part of the whole, an inexhaustible biodiversity inviting us.

### XXVIII. The River's Promise

The river, with its unwavering flow, speaks of promises, of paths leading toward the sea, unending journeys, it's the earth in motion, teaching us through movement, that life is a voyage, with lessons that kiss us.

### XXIX. The Wisdom of Seasons

Seasons, perpetually changing, speak of cycles, of constant renewal, the rhythm of time, the earth transforms, offering wisdom, that everything changes, and in change, we grow.

### XXX. The Whisper of the Desert

The desert, vast and silent, speaks of introspection, of seeking the soul, encountering essence, it challenges us, its emptiness urging us, to find fullness within its void.

### XXXI. The Strength of Granite

Granite, unyielding and eternal, speaks of resilience, the fortitude to withstand time's assaults, the enduring earth inspires us, to be unbreakable, eternal in our resistance.

### XXXII. The Mystery of Dawn

Dawn, with its light and magic, hints at mysteries, beginnings that bring hope, dreams awakened, the earth illuminates, promising, that after darkness, light always arrives.

### XXXIII. The Twilight's Refuge

Twilight, with its hues and tranquility, offers refuge, the calm we crave, the rest we deserve, the earth prepares, inviting us to find solace, in its stillness, the comfort we seek.

## XXXIV. The Song of Fire

The fire that burns within the earth, in the heart of volcanoes, is the voice of creation, the origin of lands and seas, in its fervor, the passion of the earth is revealed, and in its warmth, the history of humanity is recounted.

## XXXV. The Caress of Air

The air we breathe, which caresses the skin and soul, is the breath of the earth, its gift, its calm, with each breeze, the whisper of life is felt, and in its touch, the connection with the world becomes evident.

### XXXVI. The Embrace of Winter

Winter, with its white mantle and penetrating cold, is the earth's embrace, its rest, its moment, in its silence, the promise of spring is kept, and in its stillness, hope rises within our hearts.

### XXXVII. The Renewal of Spring

Spring, with its explosion of colors and life, is the earth's renewal, its strength, its measure, with every blooming flower, rebirth is celebrated, and in its greenness, eternal youth is revealed.

### XXXVIII. The Splendor of Summer

Summer, with its scorching sun and long days, is the splendor of the earth, its song, its praise, in its warmth, the fullness of life is felt, and in its light, the joy of living is evident.

### XXXIX. The Reflection of Autumn

Autumn, with its falling leaves and golden hues, is the reflection of the earth, its cycles, its states, in its change, preparation for rest begins, and in its palette, the beauty of life is appreciated.

### XL. The Silence of the Night

The night, with its star-studded cloak and infinite peace, is the silence of the earth, its rest, its meeting, in its darkness, the universe is contemplated, and in its calm, the human soul finds its center.

### XLI. The Hope of Dawn

Dawn, with its first light and refreshing newness, is the hope of the earth, its beginning, its test, with its birth, a new day is announced, and in its clarity, the promise of life is proclaimed.

### XLII. The Legacy of the Earth

The earth, with its history and life, bequeaths us a legacy, a message written in the wind, in the rocks, in the sea, it promises that even as time passes, we endure, in the memory of the world, in its eternal turning.

### XLIII. The Awakening of Consciousness

In the awakening of consciousness, the earth calls to us, to be more than mere spectators, to be guardians, it is the responsibility we share, the flame, that binds us in caring for our home, its valleys.

### XLIV. The Journey of the Soul

The human soul, in its journey, seeks its mirror in the earth, in its quest, the earth offers its reflection, it is the path we tread, filled with learning, and with each step, the earth accompanies us in its landscape.

### XLV. The Union of Times

In the union of times—past, present, and future— the earth bears witness to our history, our path, it echoes humanity's course, steadfast and sure, reminding us that we are one in our destiny.

### XLVI. The Embrace of Eternity

In the embrace of eternity, the earth envelops us, with unconditional love, infinite patience, it is life's gift, generously bestowed upon us, and within its embrace, echoes of humanity converge, intertwine.

### XLVII. The Final Song

And thus, in the final song, earth and humanity merge, a melody resonating in the universe's soul, it is the song of life, flooding us with harmony, and in its ending, the beginning of a new verse.

## Natural Architecture

On the canvas of the earth, nature sculpts, with invisible hands, landscapes that envelop us. Mountains that touch the sky, valleys of emerald green, formations that defy gravity, nothingness.

The rocks, like sculptures, carved by time, tell ancient stories of bygone eras. Deep caves, endless abysses, mysterious places where dreams begin and end.

The canyons, earth's fissures, narrate the force of water, like river brushes tearing through rock. And in every desert, every sand dune shaped by the wind, there's a whisper of eternity, a beauty that astounds.

Glaciers, ice giants, guardians of the cold, advance and retreat in a somber dance. Their blue tongues reflect the sun, and in their slow movement, they recount the tale of the poles.

The jungle, with its leafy canopy, a living roof, is a temple of life where biodiversity thrives. In every vine, every flower, every creature that glides, there's a verse of the earth, a mesmerizing rhyme.

Coral reefs, underwater gardens, with their vibrant colors, invite us to dream. A separate world where silence speaks, and each fish, each anemone, is a storytelling masterpiece.

Such is natural architecture—majestic and eternal, a legacy of the earth that governs our every step. May the verses of these formations sing of creation, and as you read them, may you feel passion and admiration.

For in every landscape, in every corner of the world, there's hidden poetry, a profound sentiment. May the echoes of natural architecture resonate in your heart, inspiring you to love the earth with devotion.

Let us continue our journey through natural architecture, a hymn to the earth, where each formation becomes a verse, Fiords, with their crystal-clear waters, reflect the sunlight, like mirrors of the world, revealing beauty unbridled.

Meadows, with undulating grasses, a sea of tranquility, are home to free creatures, a sanctuary of diversity. And in ancient forests, where trees touch the sky, echoes of life resound—a chorus of the earthly and the ethereal.

Volcanoes, with their internal fire, forge the earth with their might, creating islands, mountains—a legacy that endures. And on white sandy beaches, where the sea kisses the land, love stories, encounters, farewells, and wars are written.

Nature, in its infinite wisdom, has crafted a world of wonders, where each element is a poem, each detail a masterpiece.

For in every corner of the planet, there's a story to tell, a landscape that astonishes, a beauty that fuels our dreams. May the echoes of natural architecture, in their grandeur, remind us of the earth's greatness and eternal generosity.

Natural architecture, an unparalleled spectacle, is the earth's art in its most vital expression. No human hand intervenes, only the force of nature, which sculpts, paints, and creates with unwavering passion.

The pillars of the earth, the imposing mountains, are like rock cathedrals—eternal and ascending. Their peaks, like needles pointing to the sky, remind us of our smallness in the face of their mystery.

The valleys, cradles of life, embrace rivers and streams, they are the earth's masterpiece, where harmony prevails. In their fertile soils, life flourishes splendidly, and every plant, every tree, bears witness to love.

The caves, adorned with stalactites and stalagmites, are like underground chambers filled with wonders. Formed drop by drop over millennia, they serve as reminders of patience and eternal time.

The oceans, with their waves and tides, are the architects of coasts and beaches, their beauty inexhaustible. Each shell, each grain of sand, contributes to this mosaic, designed by the earth with a mesmerizing rhythm.

Natural architecture is a poem without words, the earth's voice that speaks in silence. It is a hymn to life, to continuous creation, an invitation to contemplate, to feel, to be part of this symphony.

May this poem echo the vitality of the earth, a reflection of its passion, its beauty, its unwavering strength.

Natural architecture, an unending narrative, is the living history of the earth, etched in every stone, every crevice. From flower-filled valleys to snow-capped summits, each landscape is a chapter, an illustrated page.

Geysers and thermal springs, with their ascending vapor, are like fables of the earth—an awe-inspiring spectacle. Hot water emerges from the ground, a gift from its internal heat, and within each bubble, each jet, lies an eternal tale.

River deltas, where water meets the sea, are canvases of nature where life can thrive. Rich in nutrients, these ecosystems are vital, home to birds, fish, and plants in natural harmony.

Plateaus and highlands, vast elevated expanses, offer wide panoramas—a glimpse of pure nature. They serve as balconies of the world, where the wind sings, and in their stillness, the earth reveals its sacred magic.

Mangroves, with their intertwined roots, protect the coast, acting as fortresses of life against storms—a strategic bet. Within their labyrinth of branches, biodiversity hides, and every creature, every plant, is a treasure that responds.

Natural architecture is an endless poem, a legacy of the earth that invites us to explore. May the verses of this poem lead us on an unparalleled journey, and as you read, may you feel passion, wonder, and vital love.

For in every corner of the earth, there's a wonder to discover, a landscape that leaves us breathless, a beauty beyond compare. May the echoes of natural architecture, in their diversity, inspire us to care for the earth—with passion and humility.

### The Dance of the Earth

On the world's stage, the earth dances, with movements that tell the story of hope. Mountains rise, majestic and strong, witnesses of time, defying death.

Valleys stretch out like open arms, embracing life on their covered soils. Rivers meander with clear waters, sculpting rock along their untamed paths.

Deserts extend with their golden sands, landscapes of silence where life embraces. Dunes shift to the rhythm of the wind, forming patterns in perpetual motion.

Glaciers advance, their brilliant ice, guardians of the cold in constant march. Their deep crevices conceal ancient secrets, from a frozen world beneath star-studded skies.

Forests stand tall, their trees reaching high, a green mantle that protects and captivates. Life overflows in every leaf, every branch, a hymn to nature that ignites the heart.

Each geological formation, each awe-inspiring landscape, is poetry written by the hand of shadow. The earth speaks to us with unparalleled beauty, and in its natural architecture, we find vital love.

## Earthly Meditations

In the silence of the earth, we hear its call, a whisper inviting us on an introspective journey. The earth speaks to us of roots, of deep connection, of the relationship we share, rooted in our hearts.

We are children of the earth, born from its clay and breath, finding our own place within its vastness. It teaches us humility, to value what we have, to care for its gifts, to respect its lands.

We reflect on our footprint, the mark we leave, with every step we take, on the paths we trace. The earth reminds us that everything is transient, that we must be stewards of its vital balance.

We meditate on its beauty—the simplicity of a flower, the complexity of a forest, the cycle of love. The earth is a mirror reflecting back our nature, our essence revealed in its quiet gaze.

May these earthly meditations bridge our consciousness, inviting reflection and coherence in our lives. As readers delve into these poems, may they feel inspired, to honor the earth, to live in alignment.

For within the earth lies our history, our present, our future, and in caring for it, we find a secure path. May these earthly meditations guide our journey, and may our relationship with the earth always be an act of love.

In the stillness of the earth, we find our reflection, a place for introspection, a space for counsel. The earth, with its patience, teaches us to listen, to understand life's cycles, to respect and love.

Each tree, each stone, each flowing river, is a silent teacher leading us toward reflection. They show us the way, guiding us with wisdom, reminding us that we are part of the earth, each day.

We meditate on connection, on the web of life, considering how our actions can build or destroy. The earth asks for care, attention, and tenderness, to preserve its beauty, its balance, its destiny.

We reflect in silence, amidst nature's calm, finding answers, peace, and newfound certainty. May our relationship with the earth be reciprocal, a cycle of giving and receiving, sustainable and whole.

May these earthly meditations be a call to action, to live consciously, with love and passion. As we contemplate the earth, its grandeur and mystery, may we feel inspired to care for it with unwavering commitment.

For within the earth lies the key to our existence, and in its care and protection, we discover our essence.

In the vastness of the cosmos, the earth is our sanctuary, an oasis of life in the planetary void. It invites us to contemplate, to cherish its creation, to be aware of its value and delicate condition.

The earth teaches us, with each sunrise, that every day is a gift, an opportunity to grow. Its cycles, its changing seasons, remind us that life is a flow, an ever-advancing current.

## Earthly Meditations

In the silence of the earth, we hear its call, a whisper inviting us on an introspective journey. The earth is our teacher, on its sacred soil, it teaches us to live in balance, to stand by its side.

We reflect on our essence, on what truly matters, on our connection with the earth, comforting our souls. The earth asks us to be its allies, to protect its beauty, to be responsible, not forgotten.

In the vastness of the universe, the earth is a murmur, a refuge of life, a miracle that is not abrupt. It invites us to reflection, to understand our place, in this blue and green home, at this point in the sea.

With grace, the earth teaches us about change, about adaptation, growth, challenge, and range. It shows us that life is a web of relationships, where each being, each element, has its own function.

We meditate on interdependence, on how everything is connected, how the earth sustains us, how everything is affected. The earth calls for consciousness, for us to be part of the solution, to live intentionally, compassionately, devotedly.

We reflect in stillness, drawing wisdom from nature, learning how to act skillfully. The earth is a sanctuary of knowledge, an open book teaching us to live in harmony, to become experts.

May these earthly meditations be an inner journey, a quest for meaning, for a greater purpose. As readers delve into these poems, may they find inspiration, to live in connection with the earth, with genuine passion.

For within the earth lies our essence, our reason for being, and in caring for it, we discover our duty. May these earthly meditations sing to the heart, and may our relationship with the earth always be our song.

## Desire Meditation

In the silence of the mind, where thoughts rest, lies desire—a flame that never extinguishes. It is the force that propels us, that leads us to dream, a deep longing inviting us to seek.

We meditate on desire, on its power and fire, on how it motivates us, how it becomes our game. It whispers from the soul, a voice that never fades, guiding us forward through life's unfolding.

Desire is like the wind, impossible to capture, free and wild, defying confinement. It teaches us about freedom, about true passion, about following our hearts in this transient existence.

We reflect on its essence, on the meditation of wanting, finding equilibrium, learning when to yield. Desire moves us, but it shouldn't control us, it's a companion on our journey, not a tyrant to dominate.

May this desire meditation be a path of light, a reminder that love is the crossroads of life. As readers delve into this poem, may they find clarity, within their own desires, within their own truth.

For within desire lies the spark, the inspiration, and in understanding and tending to it, we find direction. May this desire meditation sing to the heart, leading us to live with fullness, with passion.

## Serenity Meditation

In the calm of the soul, where peace settles, we find serenity—a stillness that nourishes. It becomes the spirit's refuge, a safe harbor, where the chaotic seas lose their harshness.

We meditate on serenity, on its gentle embrace, how it envelops us, creating space. It soothes the heart, a caress for pain, helping us find center, encouraging growth.

Silence is its language, tranquility its message, teaching us patience, revealing life as a journey. It shows us that within stillness lies wisdom and strength, that true rewards await in serenity's embrace.

We reflect on its essence, on the meditation of being, seeking inner peace, learning to breathe. Serenity guides us, but it shouldn't elude us, it's a state to attain, a place to inhabit.

May this serenity meditation be a path of calm, a reminder that peace resides in the soul. As readers absorb this poem, may they find solace, in their own moments of quietude, in their inner fire.

## Hope Meditation

In the dawn of each day, where light is reborn, there lies hope—a promise that never fades. It's the spark in darkness, the lighthouse in the storm, a feeling that sustains us, nourishing our souls.

We meditate on hope, on its sweet power, how it lifts us, how it fosters belief. It anchors us in uncertainty, breathes life into adversity, impelling us forward with determination and clarity.

Hope is like a seed planted within the heart, germinating patiently, blooming undeterred. It teaches us resilience, the strength of spirit, to maintain faith even when the path is rugged.

We reflect on its essence, on the meditation of what lies ahead, finding light within ourselves, refusing to give up. Hope guides us, but it shouldn't blind us, it's a vision of possibility, not an illusion to cling to blindly.

May this hope meditation be a hymn to life, a reminder that even in difficulty, beauty resides.

### Gratitude Meditation

In the grateful heart, where appreciation blossoms, we find gratitude—a virtue that never wanes. It's the recognition of blessings, love for what we have, a feeling that enriches us, shielding us from negativity.

We meditate on gratitude, on its warm presence, how it fills us with joy, how it defines our essence. It's a thanksgiving to life, to every lived moment, teaching us to value, to take nothing for granted.

Gratitude is like the sun, illuminating our days, giving strength, guiding us in harmony. It teaches us generosity, the power of giving, to appreciate the small things that make us resonate.

We reflect on its essence, on the meditation of giving thanks, finding beauty in everything, learning to recognize. Gratitude inspires us, but it shouldn't limit us, it's a starting point for cultivating more love.

May this gratitude meditation be an ode to the present, a reminder that being thankful is courageous in life.

### Time Meditation

In the constant flow of time, where moments slip away, there lies the meditation of time—a river that never restrains. It is the current of existence, the cycle of life and death, a process that carries us, teaching us about fate.

We meditate on time, on its unceasing march, how it transforms us, how it becomes our ark. It bears witness to change, a reminder that everything flows, inviting us to appreciate the now, to live what it bestows.

Time is like the air, invisible yet felt, present in every sunrise, every moment we've dwelt. It teaches us impermanence, the beauty of the instant, to savor each second before it slips away, persistent.

We reflect on its essence, on the meditation of being, finding meaning in the present, learning to grow. Time challenges us, but it shouldn't overwhelm, it's a companion on our journey, not an adversary to face.

May this time meditation be an anthem to the present, a reminder that each moment in life holds significance.

### Inspiration Meditation

In the whisper of the muse, where ideas take root, lies inspiration—a light that illuminates our pursuit. It's the breath of creativity, the impulse to create, a spark of brilliance that beckons us to contemplate.

We meditate on inspiration, its transformative might, how it opens doors, propels us in our flight. A divine spark, a gift from the universe's embrace, leading us to action, our artistic visions to trace.

Inspiration is like a melody resonating in the soul, urging expression, sharing what makes us whole. It teaches us connection, the union of mind and heart, finding our voice within the vast song's art.

We reflect on its essence, in the meditation of creation, seeking passion in our work, learning to soar with elation. Inspiration challenges us, but need not overwhelm, it's a path to beauty, not a burden to helm. May this meditation on inspiration be an anthem to imagination, a reminder that in life, creation is our finest dedication.

### Silence Meditation

In the embrace of silence, where words cease to exist, lies depth—an ocean that gently kisses our soul's mist. It's the refuge of the spirit, the space between each sound, a sanctuary of calm, where secrets are unbound.

We meditate within silence, exploring its richness and mystery, how it unveils truths, shapes our inner history. Like a blank canvas, it pauses life's cacophony, allowing us to hear our own symphony.

Silence is akin to night, enveloping all in its cloak, inviting introspection, urging us to evoke. It teaches us to listen, to be fully present, to find inner peace in a world so loud and absent.

We reflect on its essence, in the meditation of existence, seeking meaning in the unsaid, in silent persistence. Silence challenges us, yet need not intimidate, it's a wordless teacher, a guide to contemplate.

May this meditation on silence be a journey to the heart, a reminder that in stillness, passion finds its start. ◈◈♀❤

## Transformation Meditation

In the crucible of life, where everything renews, lies transformation—a force that ascends and imbues. It's the process of change, constant evolution, a path toward the new, a vibrant solution.

We meditate on transformation, its metamorphic might, how it reinvents us, challenges the status quo's flight. A dance of existence, a cycle of growth and decline, teaching adaptability, resilience, and design.

Transformation is like fire, purifying and renewing, its flames shaping us, an alchemy worth pursuing. It teaches courage, the art of letting go, embracing the unknown, the will to glow.

We reflect on its essence, in the meditation of becoming, finding strength in change, in defining and becoming. Transformation challenges us, yet need not intimidate, it's an opportunity to grow, to realize our truth's state.

## Consciousness Meditation

In the abyss of the mind, where secrets lie concealed, dwells consciousness—an ocean patiently revealed. It's the mirror of being, the inner light we embrace, a reflection of our essence, our intrinsic grace.

We meditate on consciousness, its unfathomable depth, how it defines us, unyielding in its breadth. At our core, it resides—the center of our existence, connecting us to the universe, to all with persistence.

Consciousness is like the cosmos—vast and mysterious, inviting exploration, unveiling its curious delirious. It teaches perception, the dance of reality and illusion, the art of intentional living, fueled by passion's fusion.

We reflect on its essence, in the meditation of knowing, seeking truth within, our inner compass showing. Challenging yet guiding, consciousness need not confuse, it's a path to wisdom, an unwavering muse.

May this meditation on consciousness be a voyage to infinity, a reminder that self-awareness is life's sacred affinity. As you read this poem, may you feel its profound weight, consciousness within, authenticity as your soul's estate.

For within consciousness lies the key—the understanding, in exploration and acceptance, our foundation expanding. May this meditation echo through the soul's expanse, leading us to live fully, with tranquility's dance.

### Existence Meditation

In the vast silence of the universe, where stars whisper, exists **existence**, an enigma that troubles us. It's the mystery of being, the unanswered question, a journey without a destination, a quest that beckons.

We meditate on existence, in its overwhelming immensity, how it defines us, how it shapes our dawn's luminosity. It's the fabric of reality, the thread of our life, connecting us to all that is, in a shared cosmic strife.

Existence is like the ocean—deep and unknown, inviting us to dive, to explore the uncomprehended zone. It teaches us about being, about our smallness and grandeur, about the importance of living consciously, with surety's allure.

We reflect on its essence, in the meditation of existence, seeking purpose in life, in the simple act of breathing persistence. Existence challenges us, yet need not overwhelm, it's an adventure toward the eternal, a daring realm.

May this meditation on existence be a voyage to infinity, a reminder that being is life's sacred affinity. As you read this poem, may you feel its profound depth, existence within your being, universality in your truth's breadth.

### Being Meditation

In the stillness of the cosmos, where time halts its flight, resides **being**, a mystery that cradles us in its light. It's the essence of life, the soul of the universe, an endless journey without origin or final verse.

We meditate on being, exploring its ethereal nature, how it connects us to all, shaping our personal signature. At our core, it resides—the spark of creation's fire, binding us to every star, every celestial choir.

Being is like light piercing through darkness, guiding us toward truth, toward authenticity's starkness. It teaches unity, our connection to existence's flow, the vital importance of living mindfully, letting our essence glow.

We reflect on its essence, in the meditation of universal being, seeking purpose in life, embracing love's unerring feeling. Being challenges us, yet need not overwhelm, it's an invitation to discover, to become what we truly helm.

## Deep Roots

On the final page of this journey, where words alight and settle, the book **"Deep Roots"** closes—a work that composes us.

It's the end of a chapter, yet not the entire tale, a moment to reflect, to recall the memory's trail.

We meditate on what we've learned, on the roots we've explored, how each poem, each verse, has transformed us, restored. They mirror our being, express our soul's refrain, leading us to travel, to discover inner terrain.

Deep roots are akin to the tree of life's grand design, growing and expanding with resolute incline. They teach us of connection, of our essence and mission, the vital importance of living with passion, with vision.

## *Reflection on Roots*

In the essence of contemplation, within the meditation of being, we seek truth within our roots, their potent decree. Roots define us, yet also beckon us to soar, to discover new horizons, to dream evermore.

As this book closes, may it be the beginning of more, a reminder that in life, each ending wears a disguise. As readers finish this journey, may they feel the connection, the roots within their being, the spirituality that lies.

For within roots lies the genesis, the identity's embrace, in exploration and acceptance, freedom finds its space.

*These reflections aim to inspire inner dialogue, inviting readers to explore the spiritual teachings of "Deep Roots" and how they resonate within their own existence.*

# Invitation to Spiritual Reflection: Deep Roots

1. **Divine Connection**: How can you find your reflection in nature and the cosmos to strengthen your spiritual connection?

1. **Introspection**: When reading "Deep Roots," what emotions and thoughts emerge about your spiritual journey?

1. **Ancestral Wisdom**: In what ways have your ancestors' teachings nourished the roots of your spiritual being?

1. **Inner Growth**: What lessons from "Deep Roots" can you apply to cultivate an internal garden of peace and wisdom?

1. **Meditation and Reflection**: Which meditative practices help you delve into the layers of your soul, as suggested by the book?

1. **Universal Harmony**: How can you contribute to life's symphony by honoring your unique place in the fabric of existence?

1. **Gratitude**: What aspects of your life inspire gratitude, and how does this reflect in your spiritual well-being?

1. **Spiritual Legacy**: What imprints do you wish to leave in the world that mirror the deep roots of your spirit?

## Author's Notes

Upon closing this book, 'Deep Roots,' I pause for a moment to reflect on the journey we have embarked upon together. Each poem has been a step further along the path of self-exploration and expression, an attempt to capture the essence of our connection with the earth and with ourselves.

The inspiration for 'Deep Roots' arose from contemplating nature and personal introspection. I have delved into the depths of the human experience to find words that resonate with the beauty and complexity of our inner and outer worlds.

The writing process has been both a challenge and a revelation. It has demanded patience, introspection, and, above all, attentive listening to the silent voice of inspiration. Each poem has been an act of love and a tribute to life in all its forms.

It is my hope that 'Deep Roots' serves as a refuge for the reader, a place to find solace, inspiration, and a deeper connection to the essence of life. May these poems be seeds that sprout in the fertile soil of your soul, giving rise to a forest of understanding and empathy.

I express gratitude to every reader who has accompanied us on this journey, allowing my words to become a part of their world. May the roots we have discovered together hold us steadfast and enable us to reach new heights in our own travels.


With gratitude and warmth


APOLO

## NAMASKARAM